HENNA WORK BOOK

LEARN DESIGNING

SUMAIYYA

ISBN 979-888555823-5

Contents

CHAPTER I

Lines

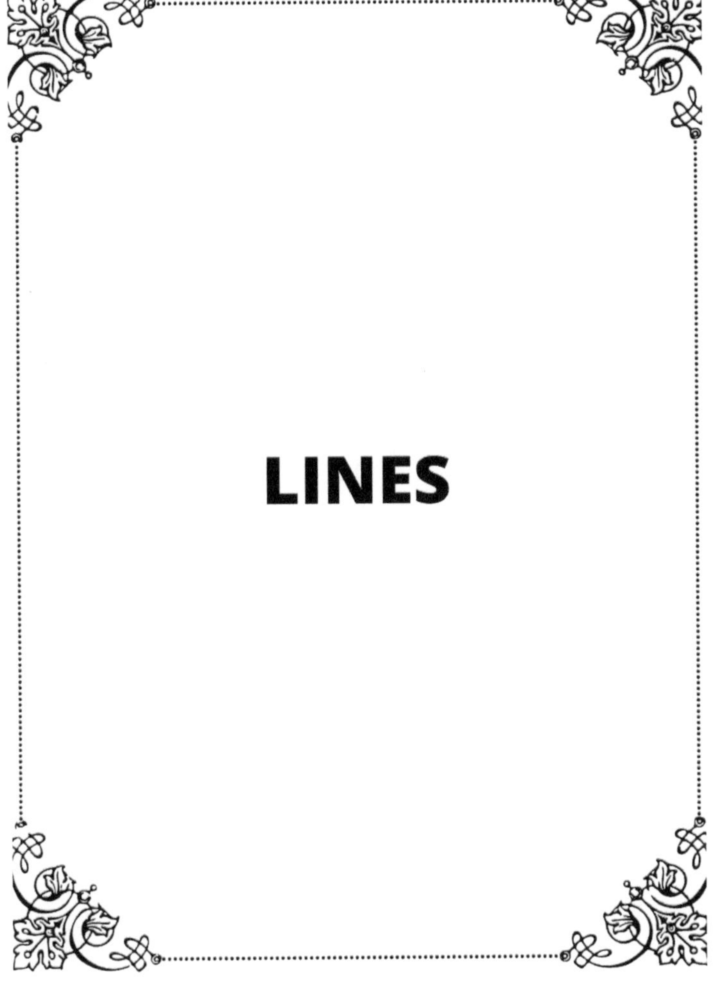

Imitate the designs in blank space to practice

Imitate the designs in blank space
to practice

Draw the line designs that you know,
except the designs given in this book

CHAPTER II

Shapes

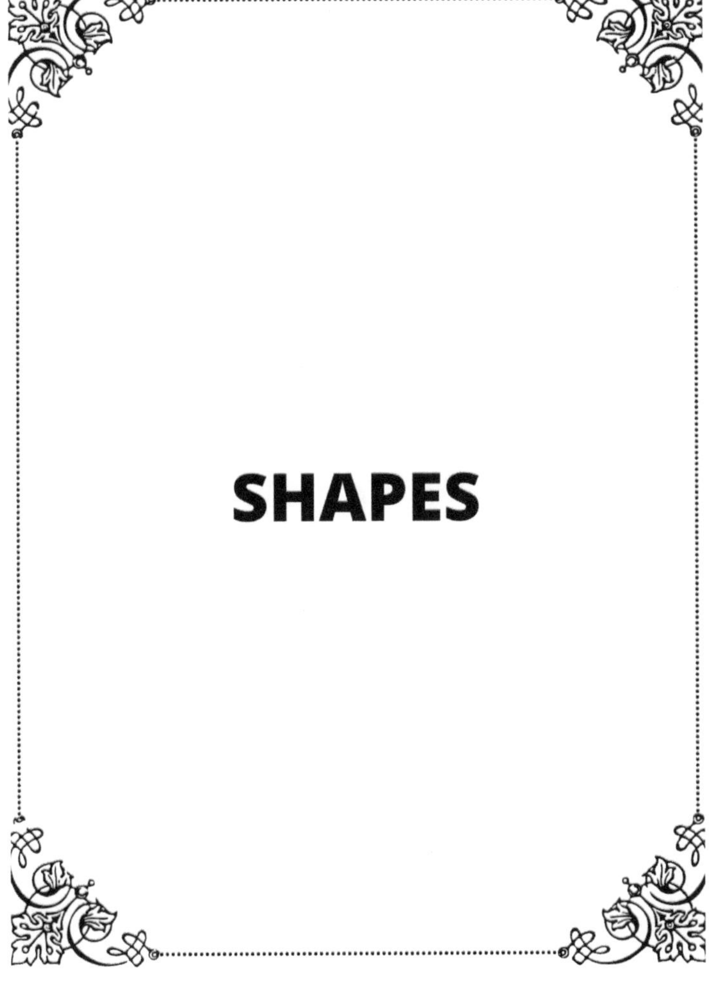

Trace on shapes

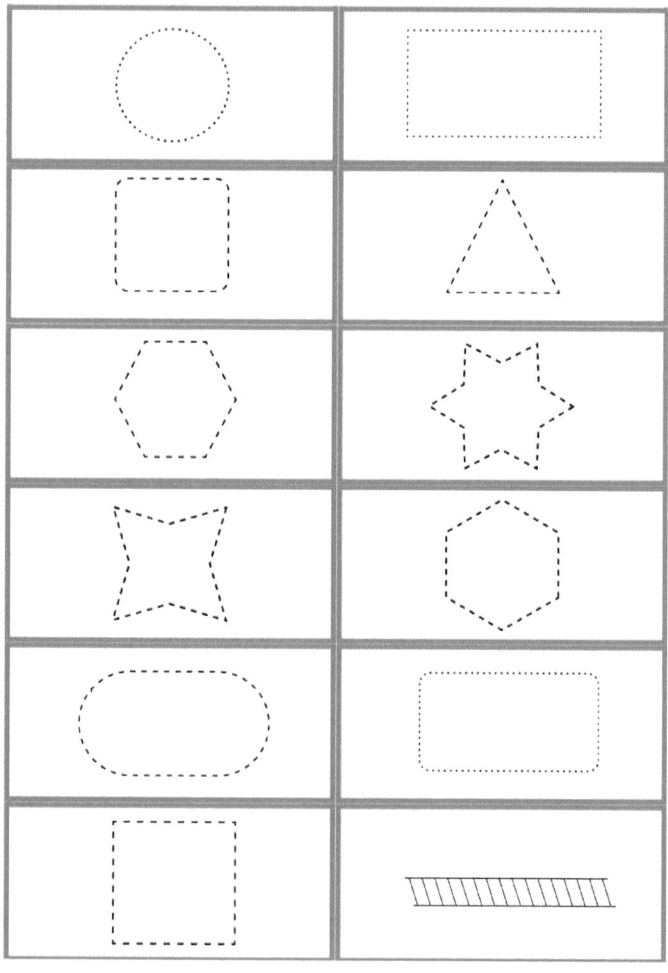

Imitate the designs in blank space
to practice

Imitate the designs in blank space to practice

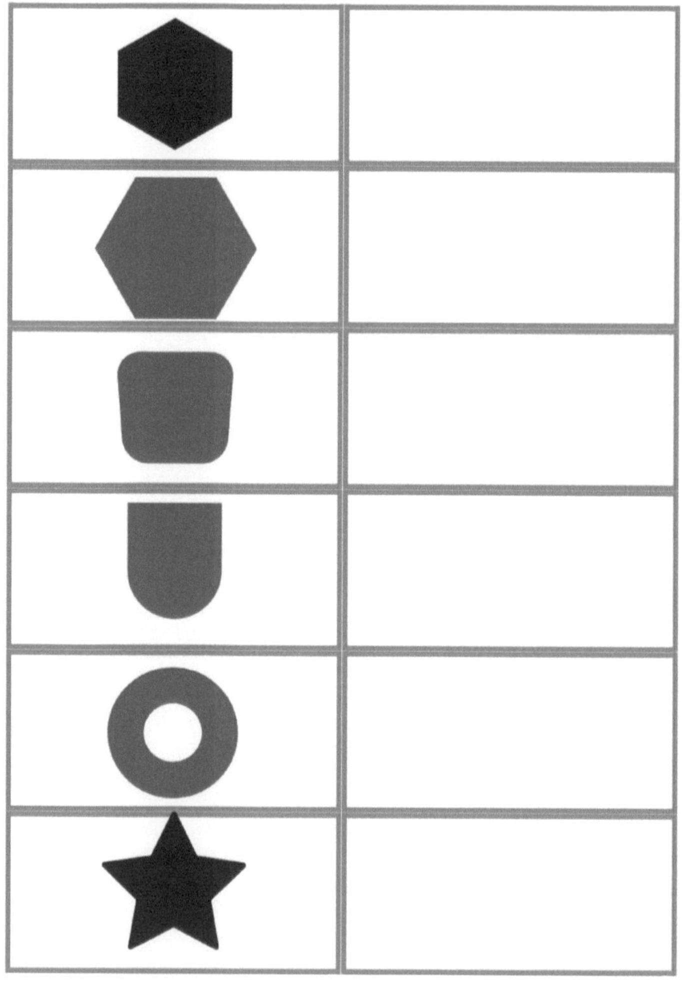

Imitate the designs in blank space
to practice

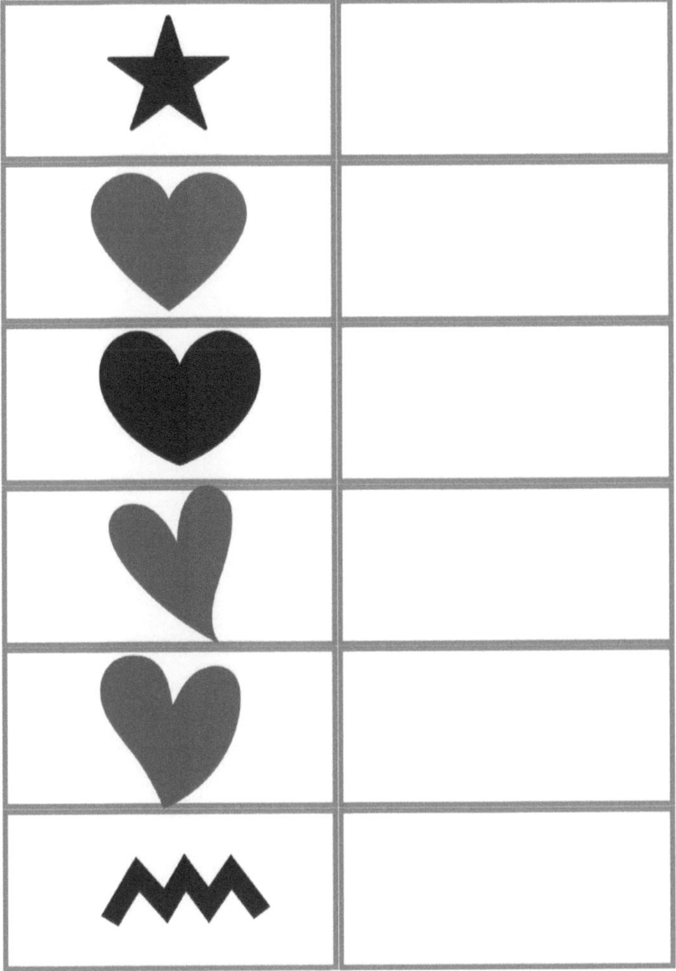

Imitate the designs in blank space to practice

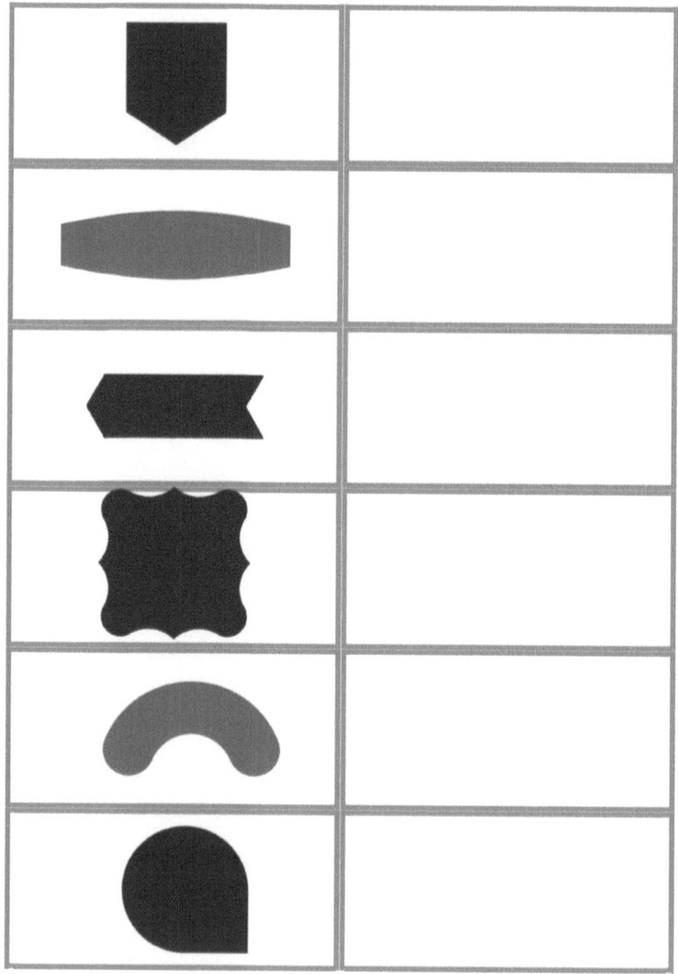

Draw the shape designs that you know,
except the designs given in this book

CHAPTER III

Circles

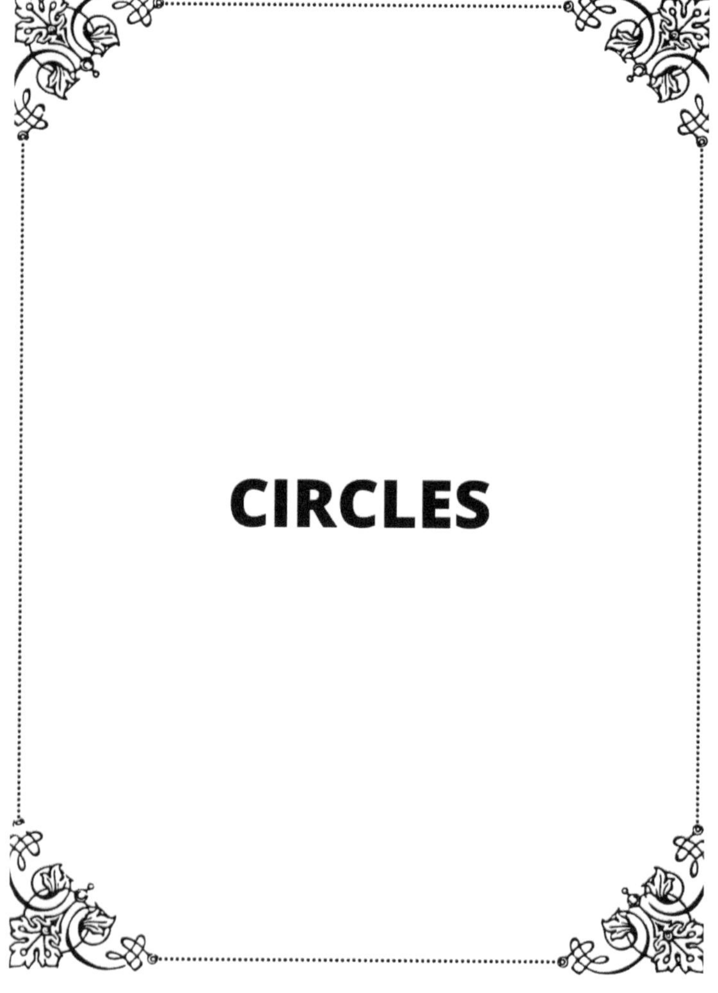

Imitate the designs in blank space to practice

Imitate the designs in blank space to practice

Imitate the designs in blank space to practice

Draw the circle designs that you know,
except the designs given in this book

CHAPTER IV

Swirls

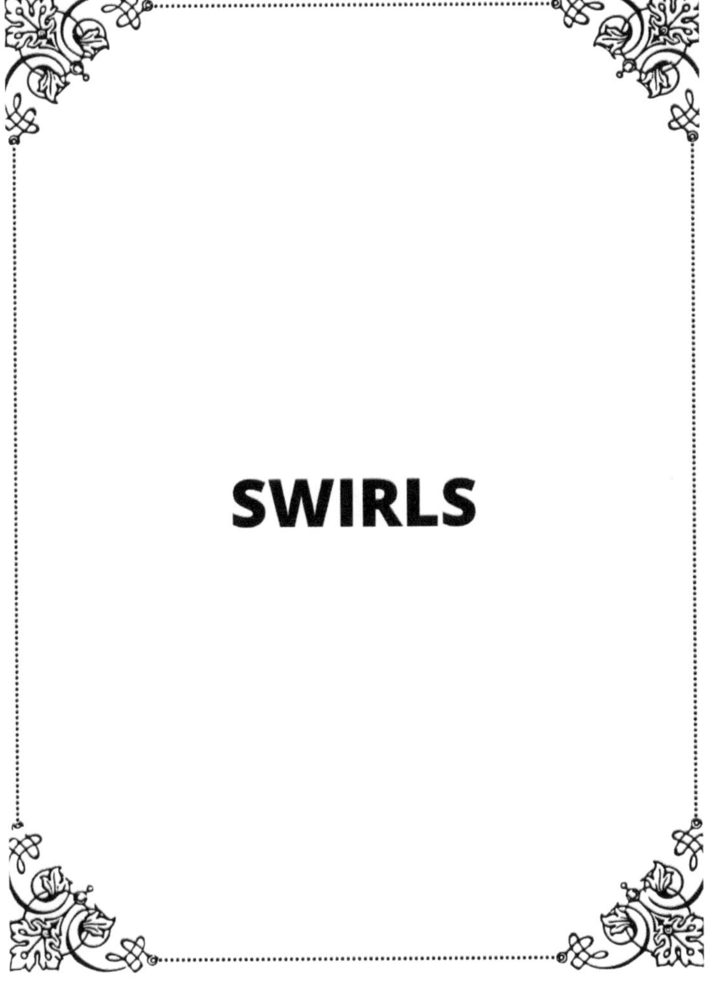

Imitate the designs in blank space to practice

Imitate the designs in blank space
to practice

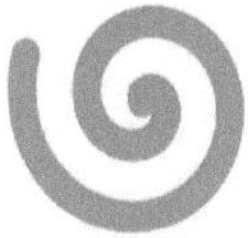

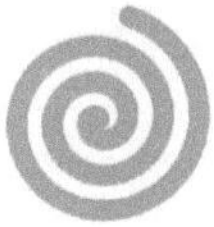

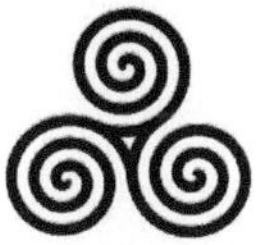

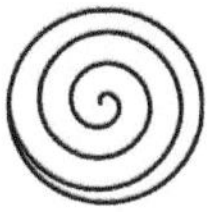

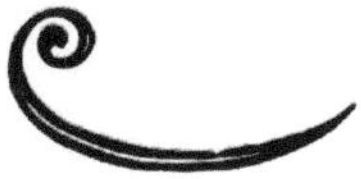

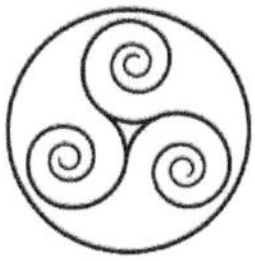

Imitate the designs in blank space to practice

Draw the swirl designs that you know,
except the designs given in this book

CHAPTER V

Curves

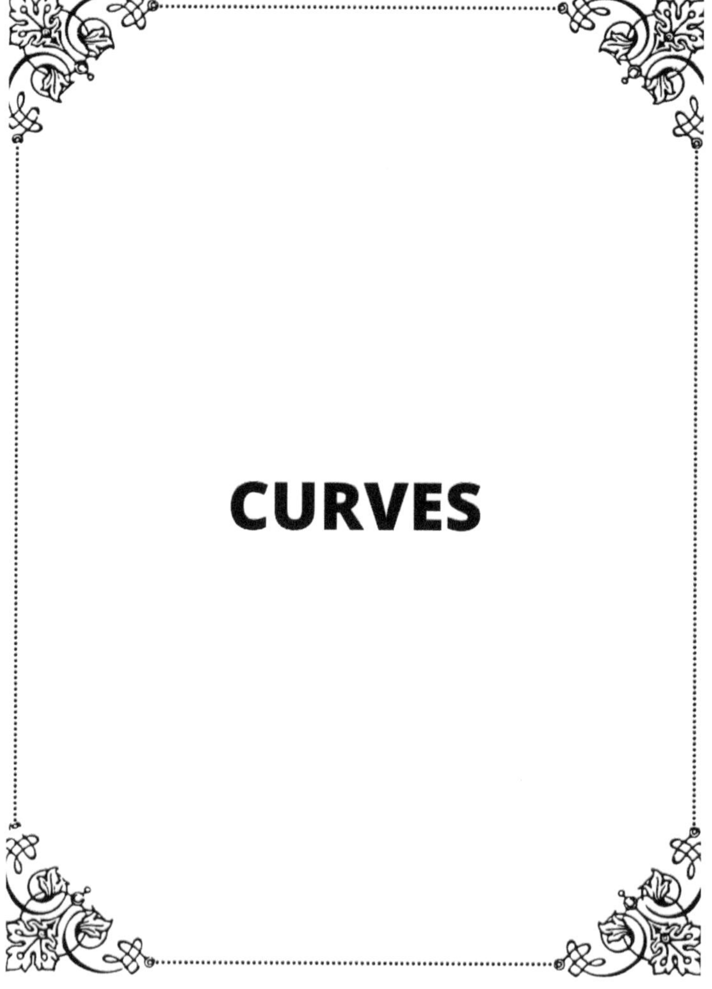

Imitate the designs in blank space
to practice

Draw the curve designs that you know,
except the designs given in this book

CHAPTER VI

Drops

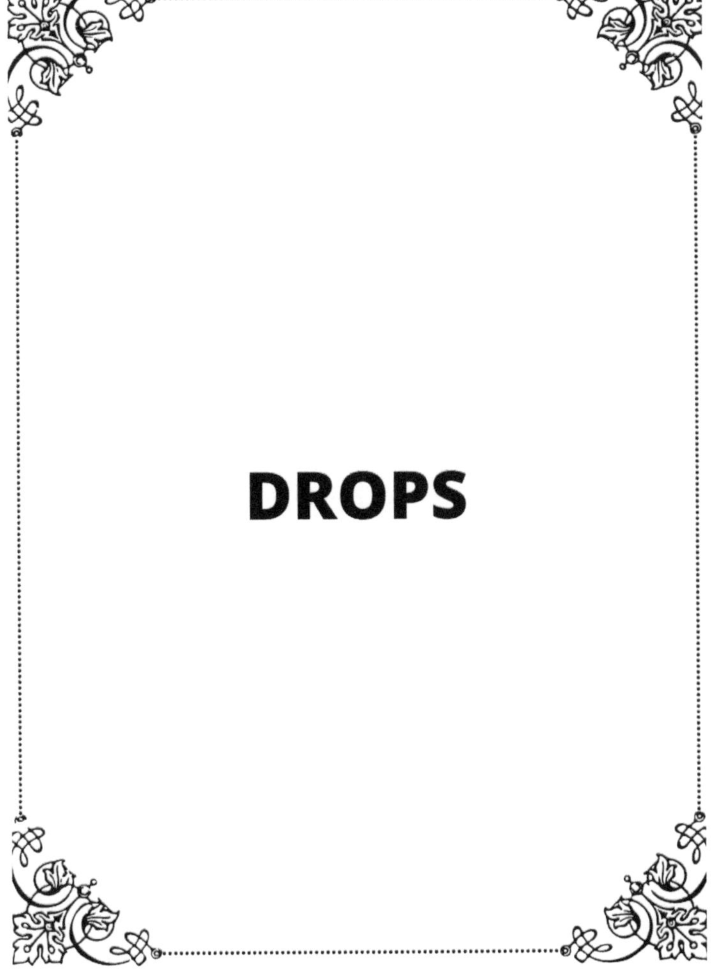

Imitate the designs in blank space to practice

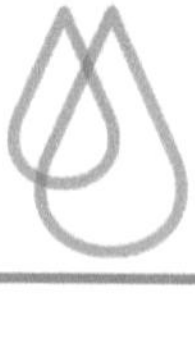	

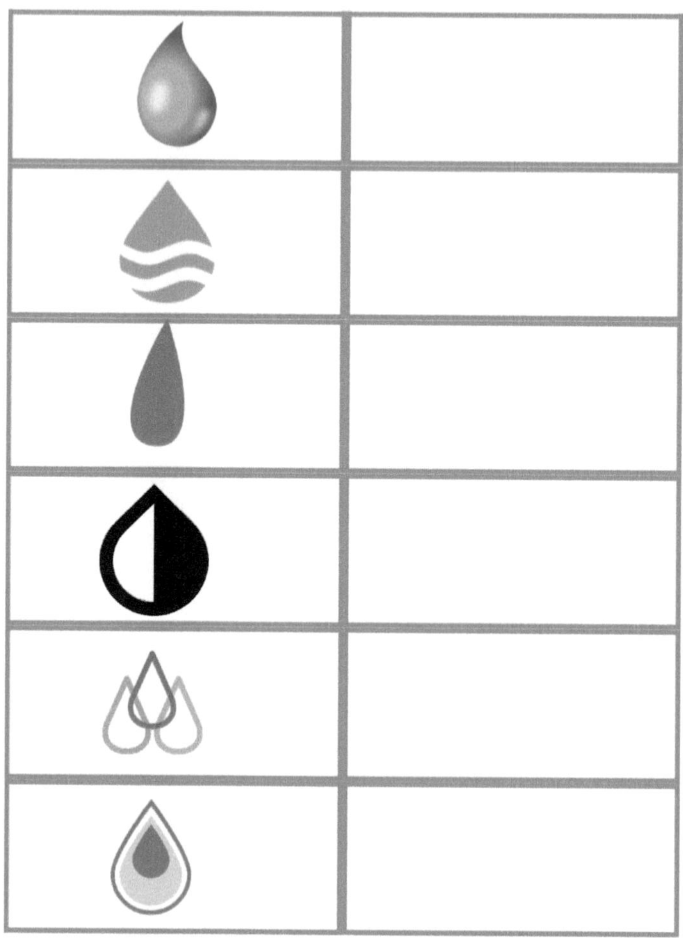

Draw the drop designs that you know,
except the designs given in this book

CHAPTER VII

Humps

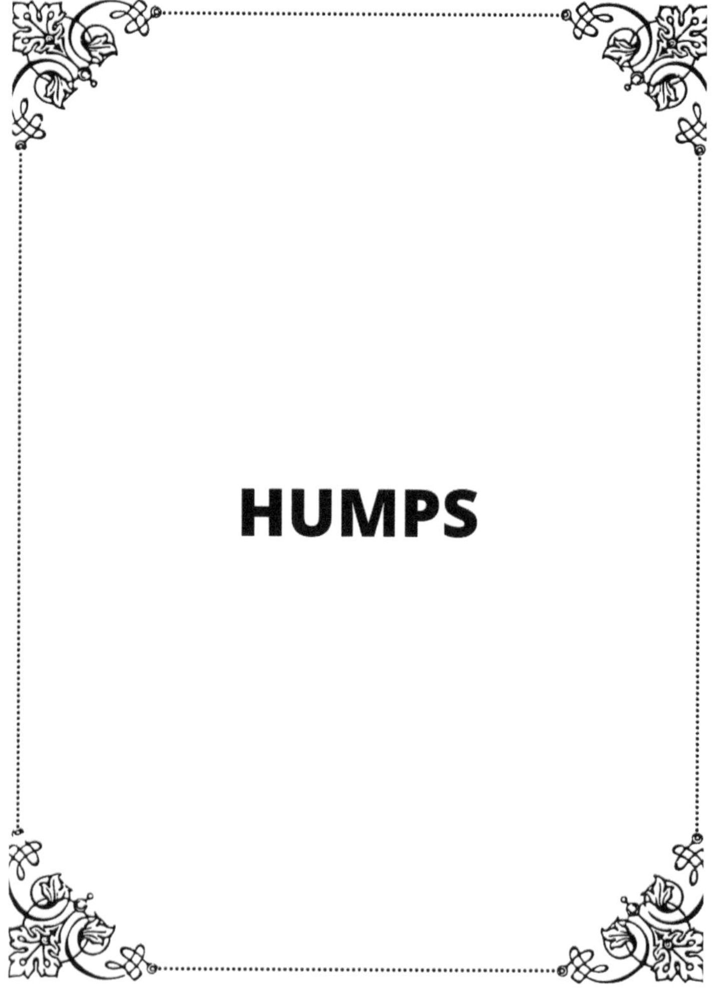

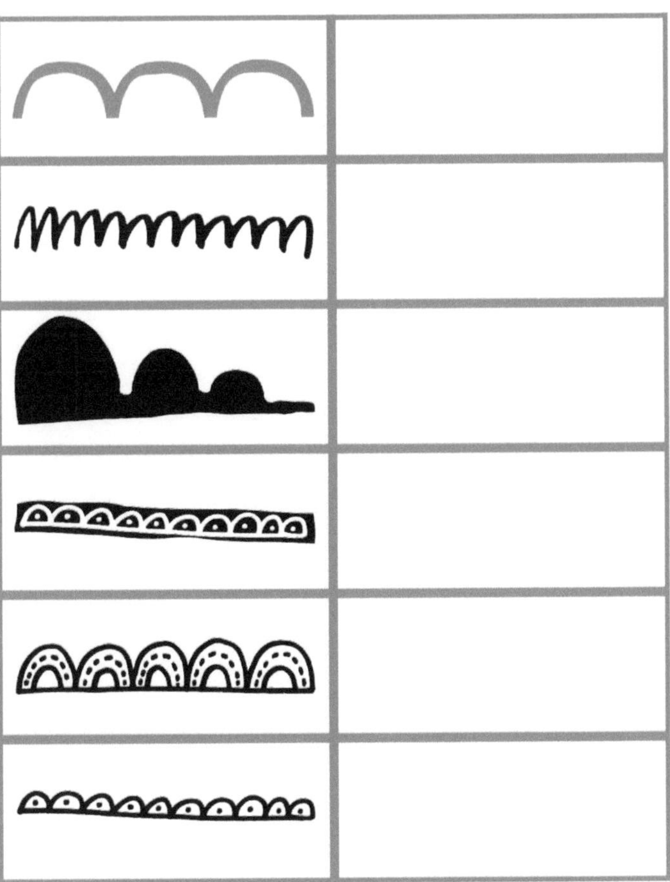

Imitate the designs in a given blank space.

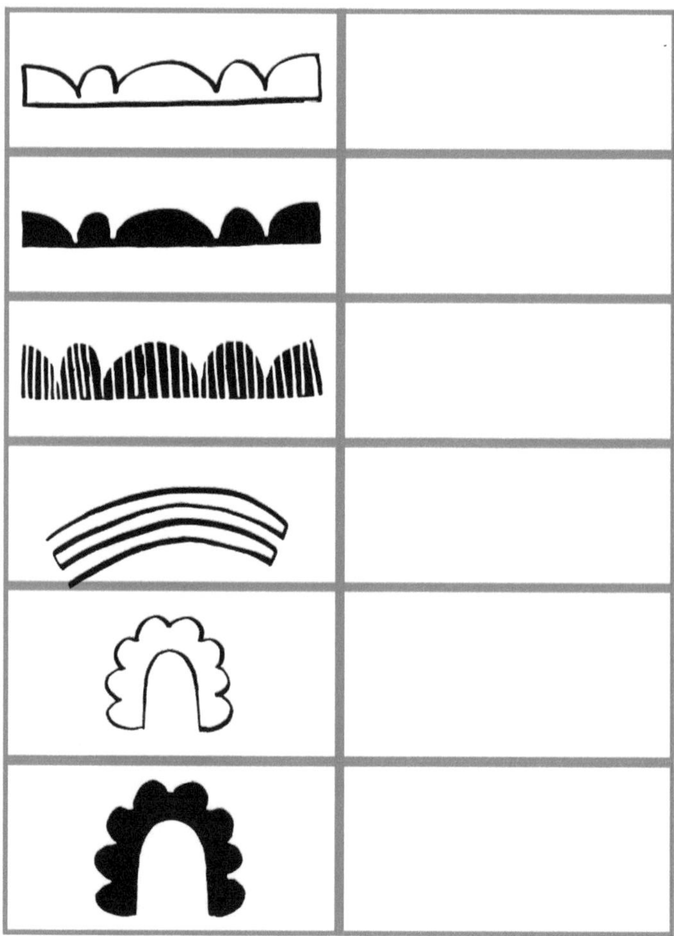

Imitate the designs in a given blank space

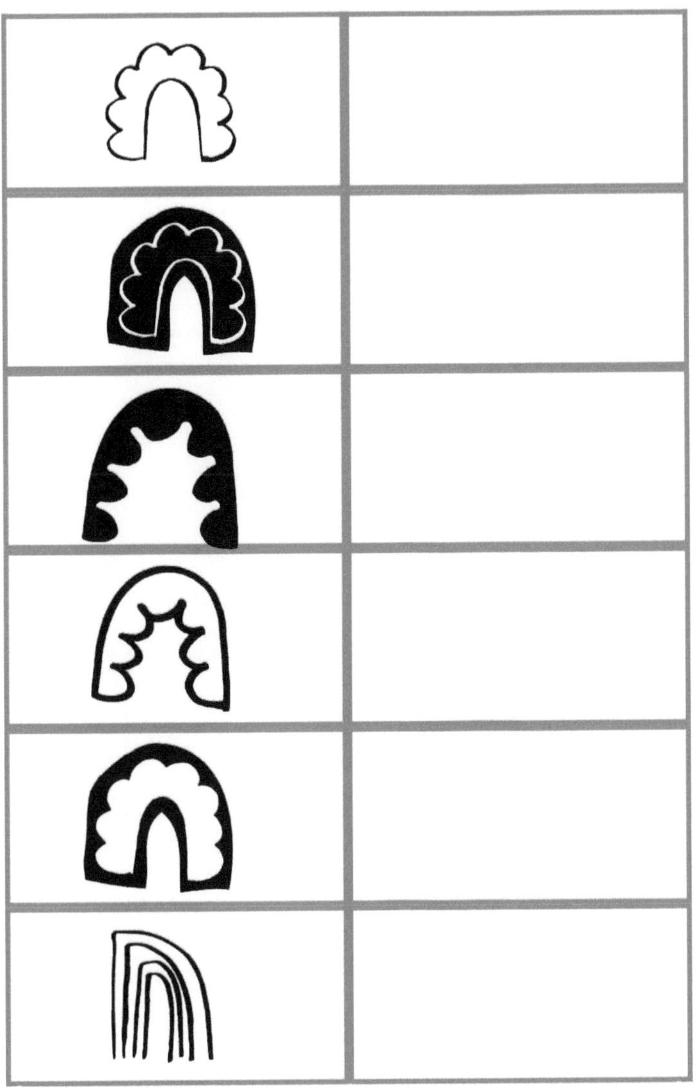

Imitate the designs in the given blank space.

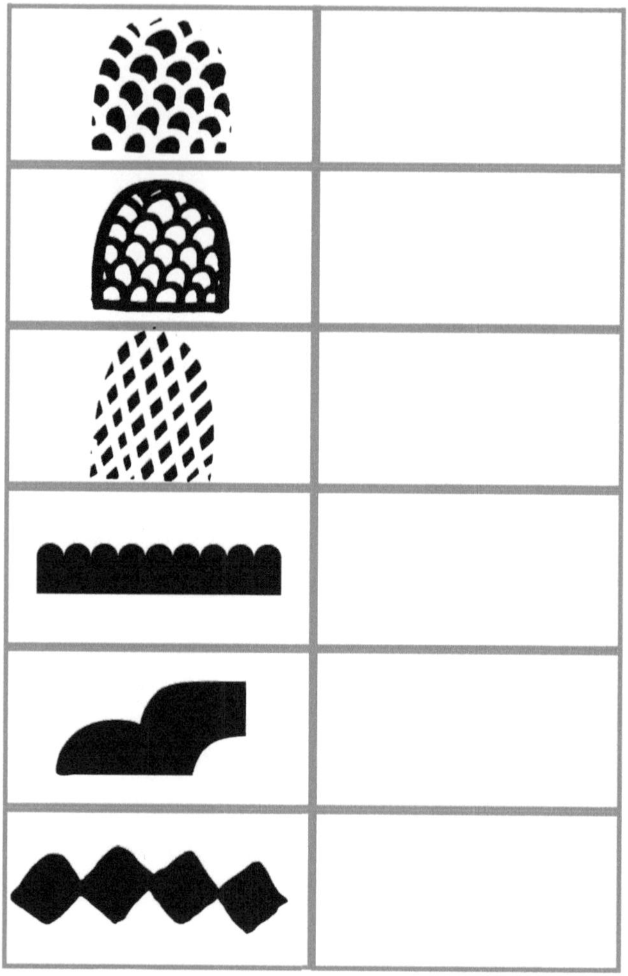

Draw the hump designs that you know,
except the designs given in this book

CHAPTER VIII

Leaves

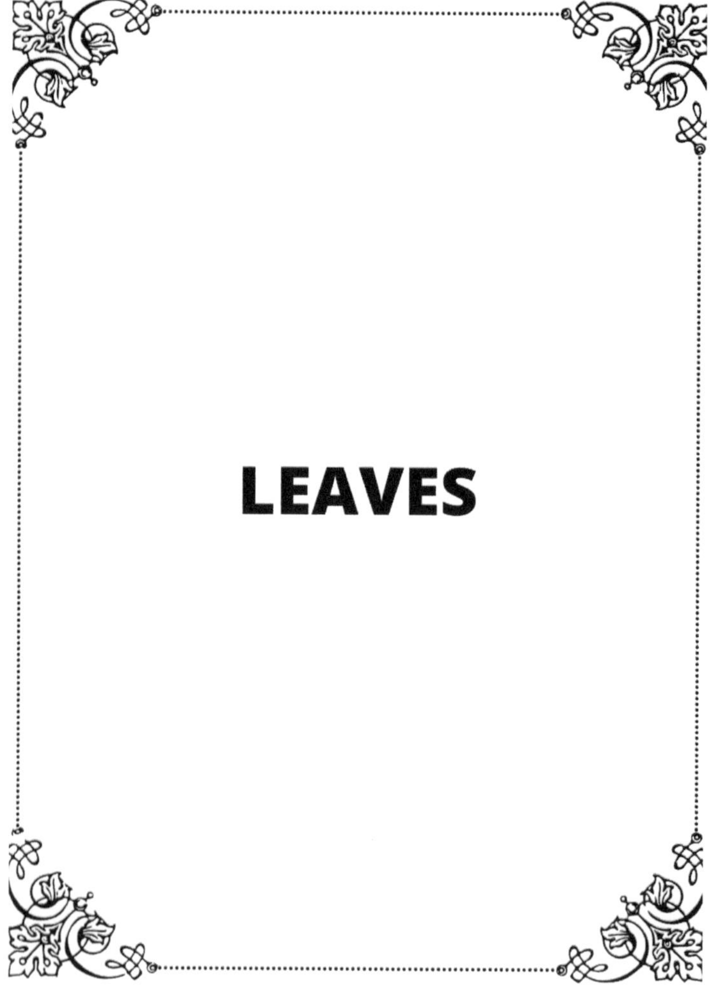

Imitate the designs in blank space to practice

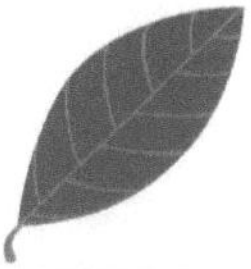	
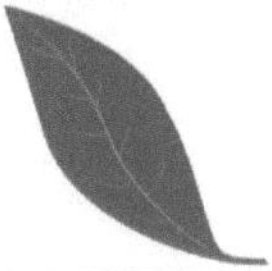	

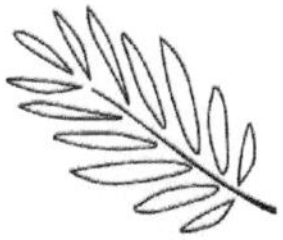	
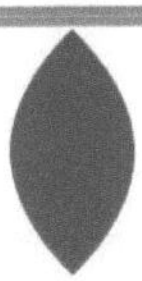	
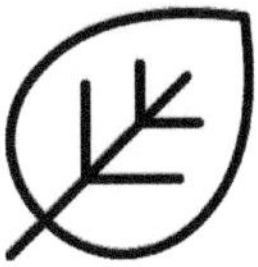	

Imitate the designs in blank space to practice

Draw the flowers that you know except the designs given in this book

Draw the flowers that you know except the designs given in this book

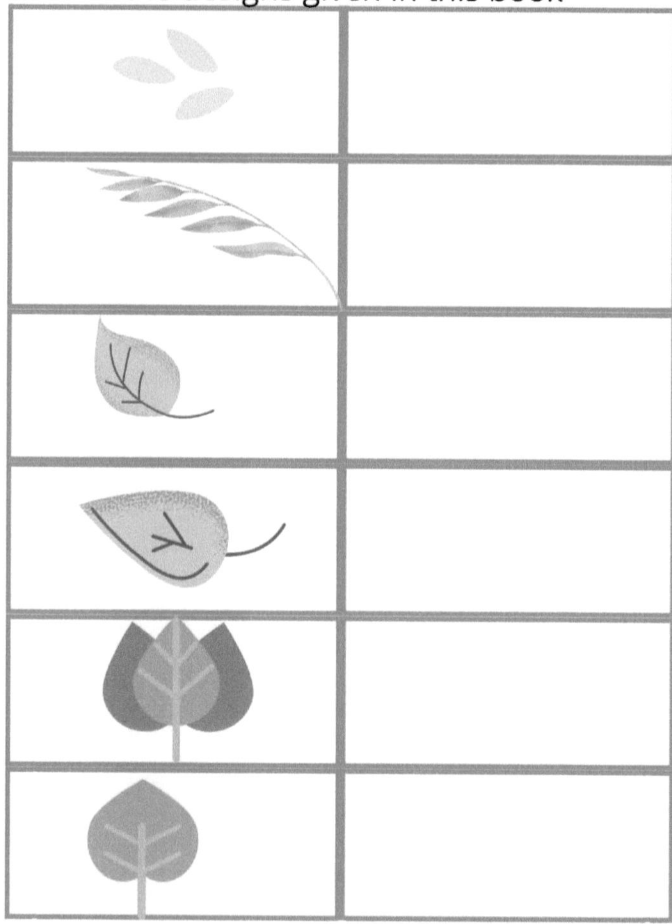

Draw the flowers that you know except the designs given in this book

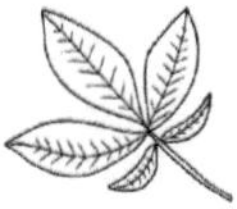	
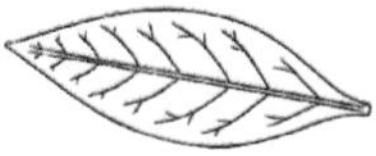	
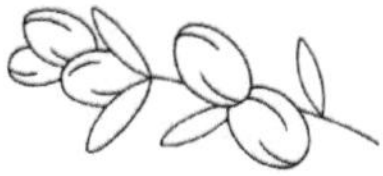	
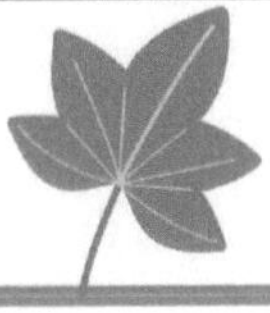	
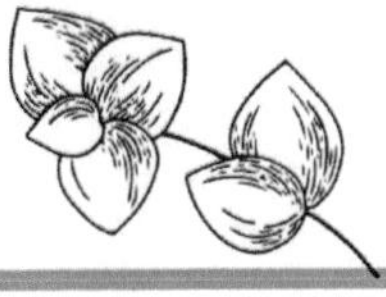	
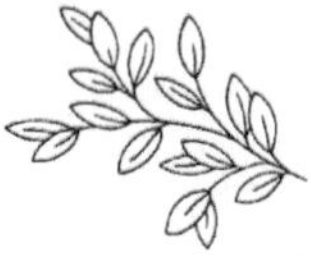	

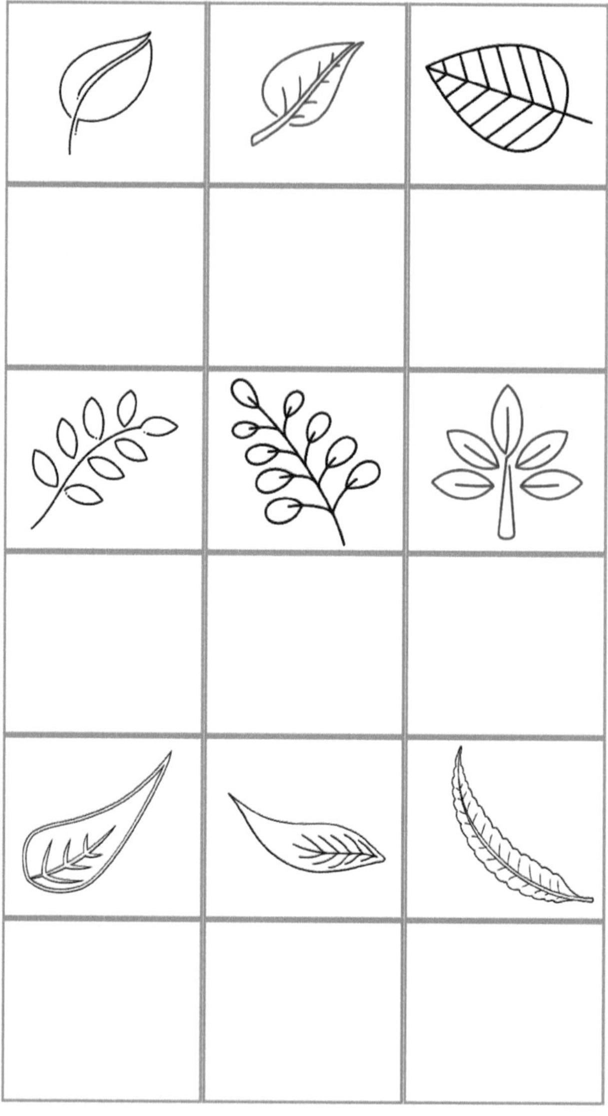

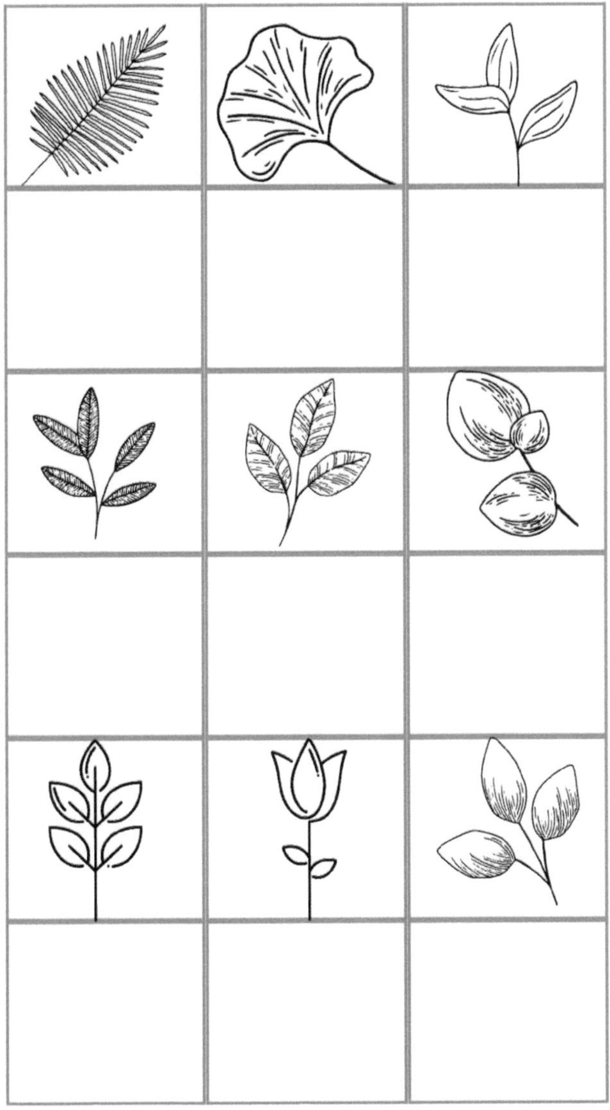

CHAPTER IX

Flowers

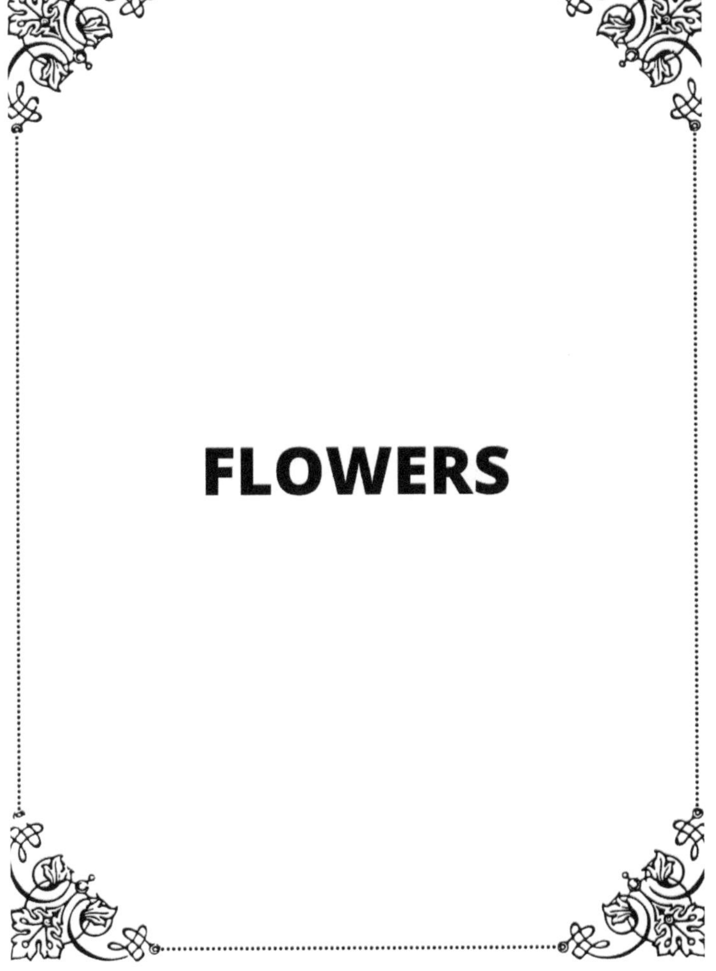

Imitate the designs in blank space to practice

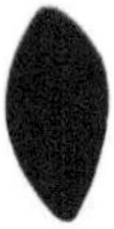	
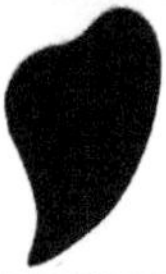	

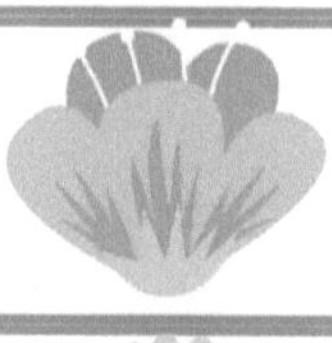	
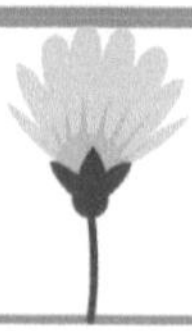	

Imitate the designs in blank space to practice

Imitate the designs in blank space to practice

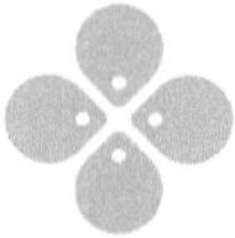	
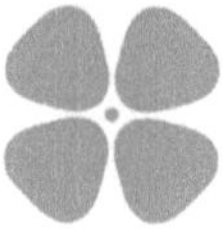	
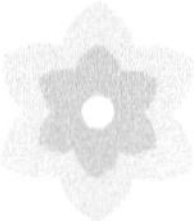	
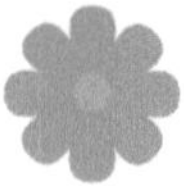	
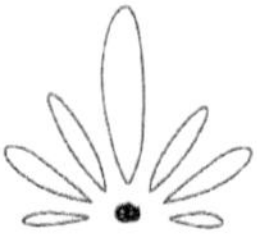	
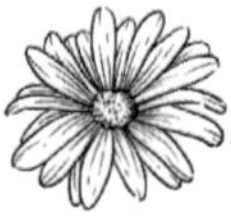	

Imitate the designs in blank space to practice

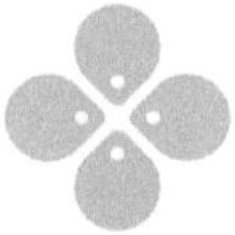	
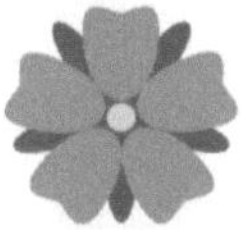	

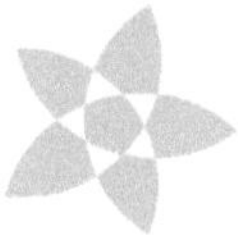	

Imitate the designs in blank space to practice

Imitate the designs in blank space to practice

Imitate the designs in blank space to practice

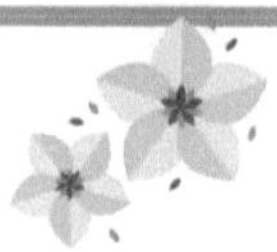	

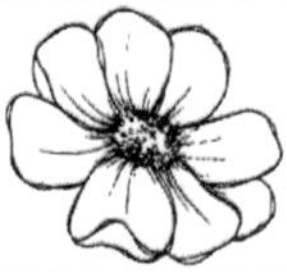	
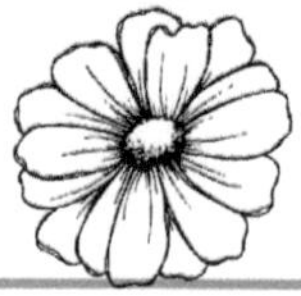	

Imitate the designs in blank space to practice

Imitate the designs in blank space to practice

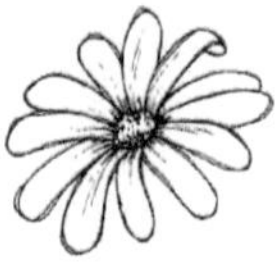	

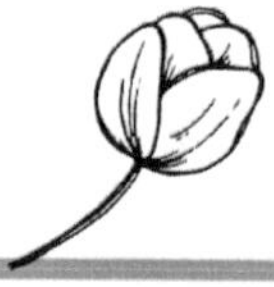	
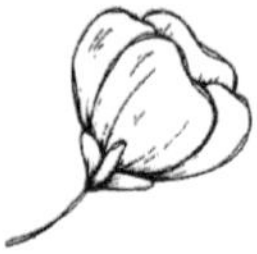	
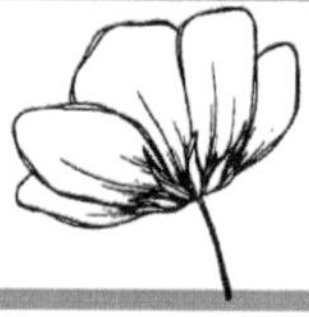	
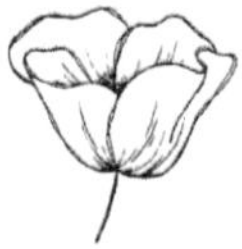	

Imitate the designs in blank space
to practice

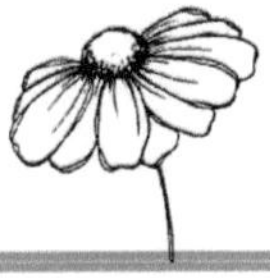	
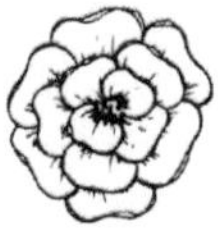	
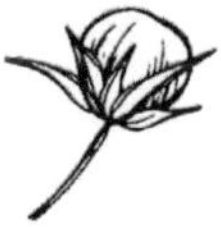	
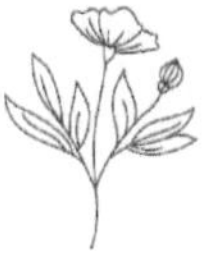	
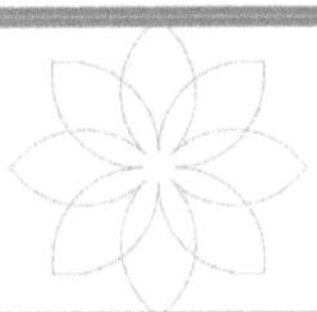	
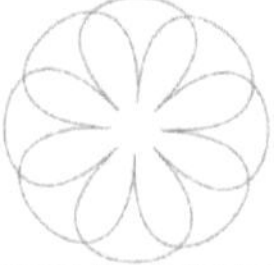	

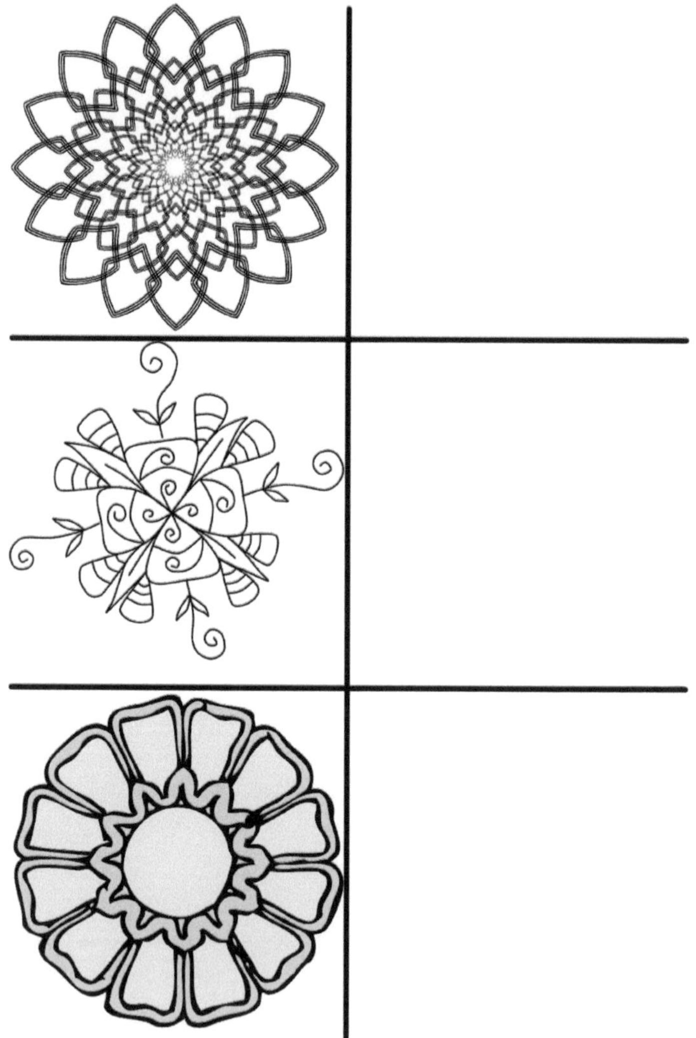

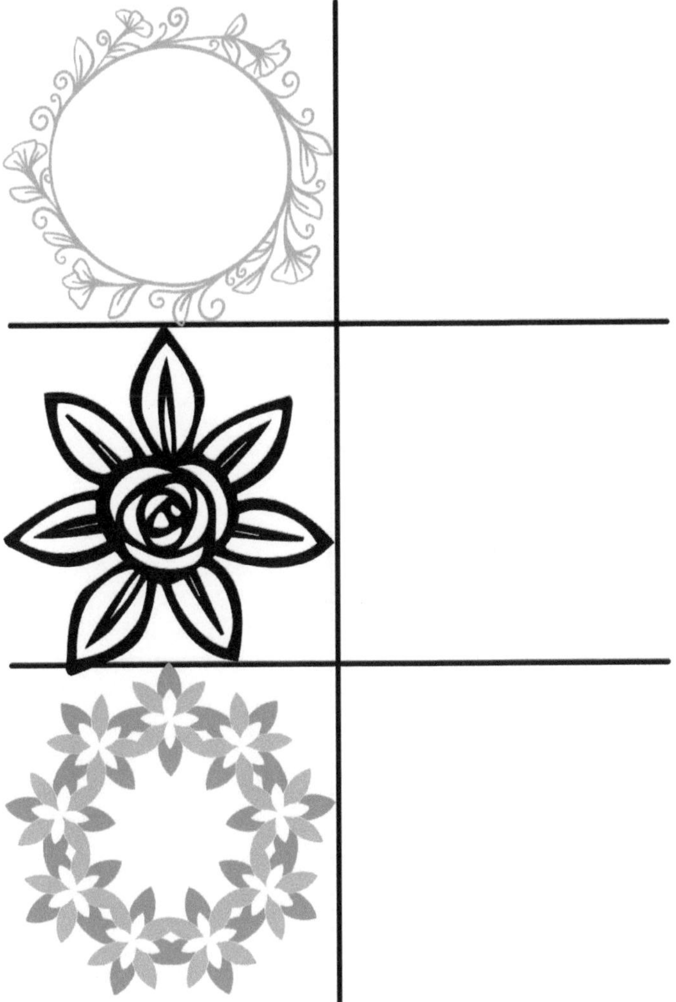

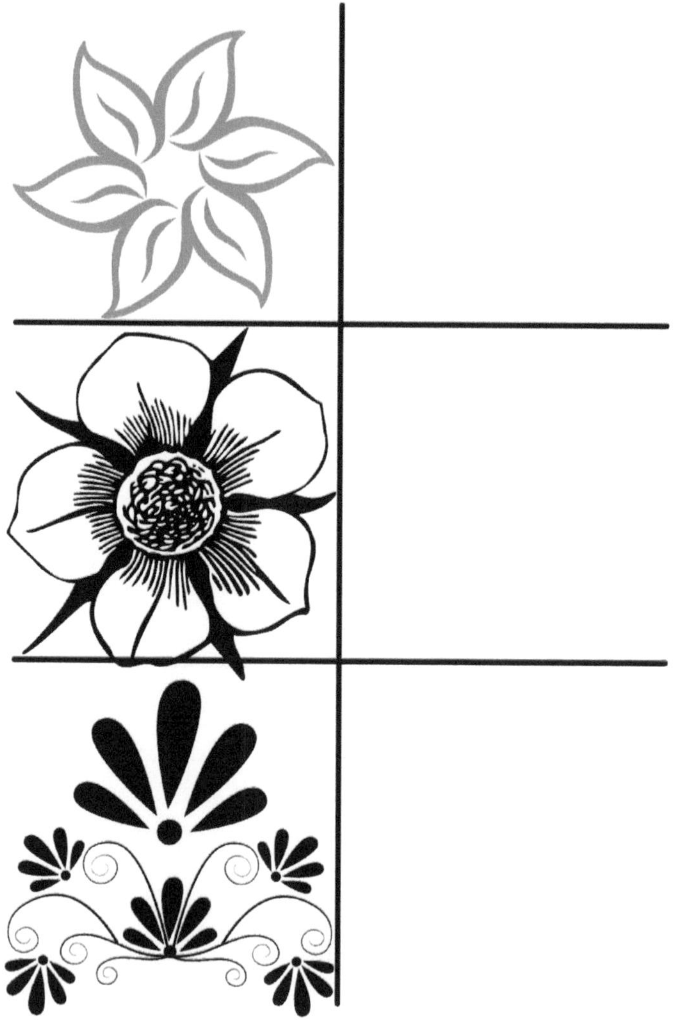

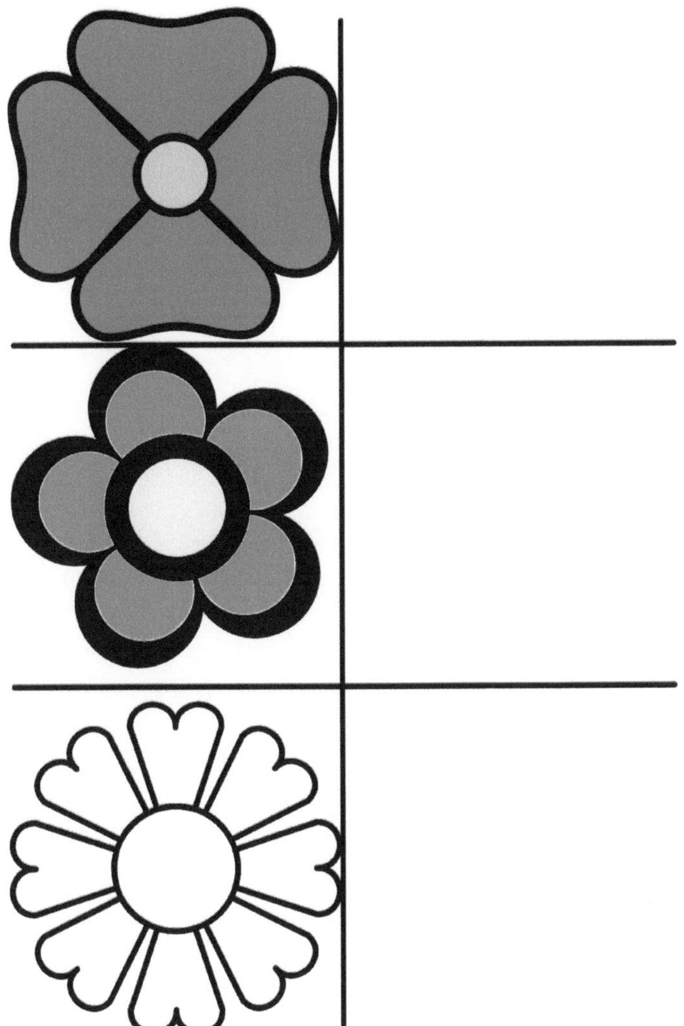

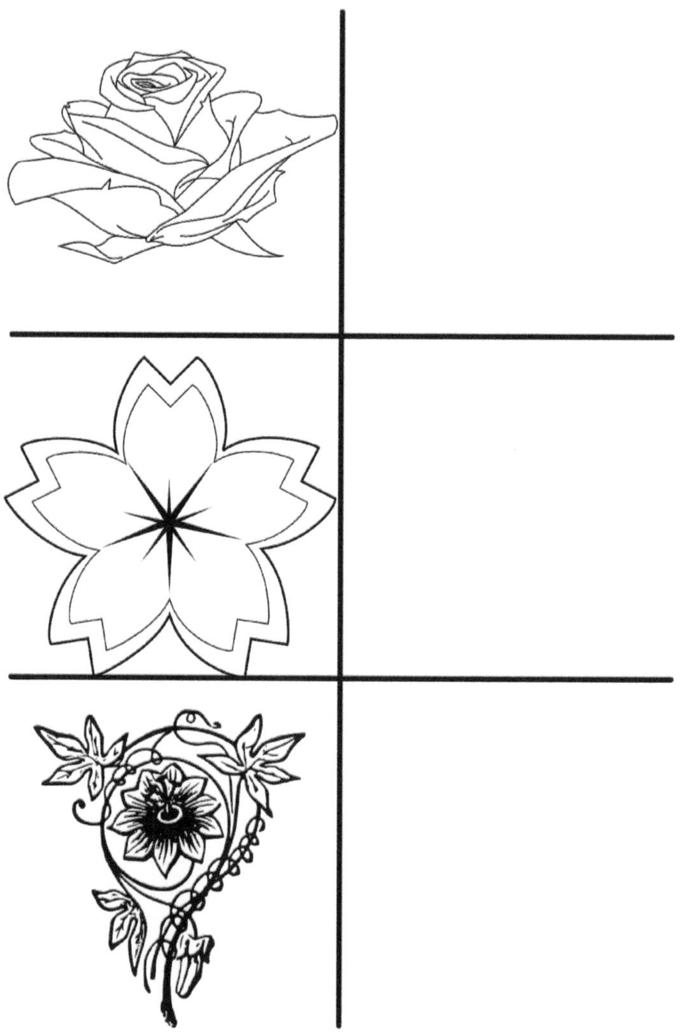

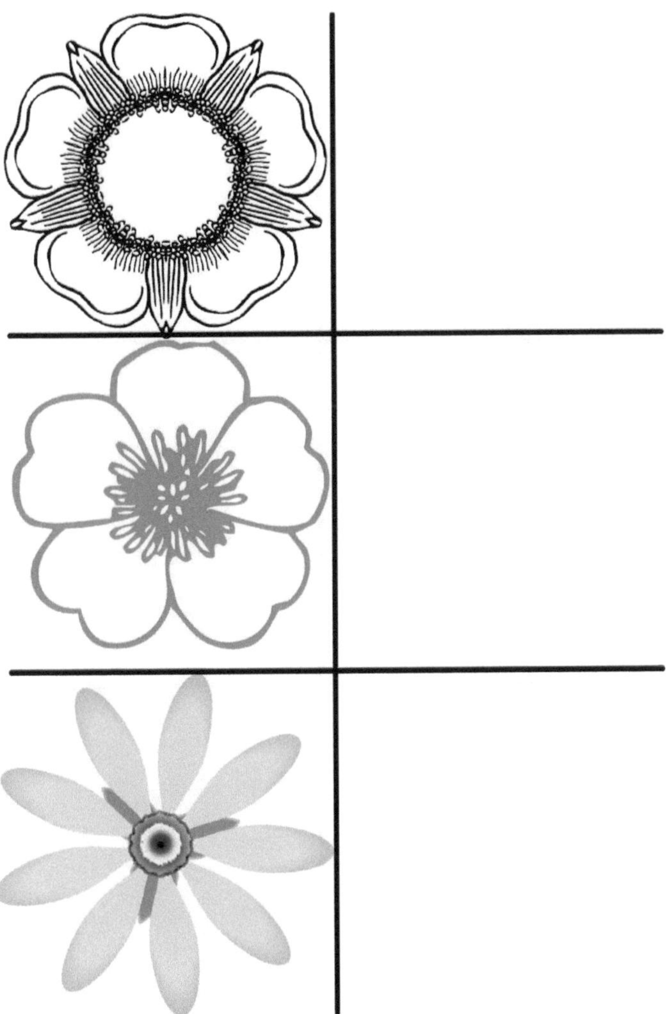

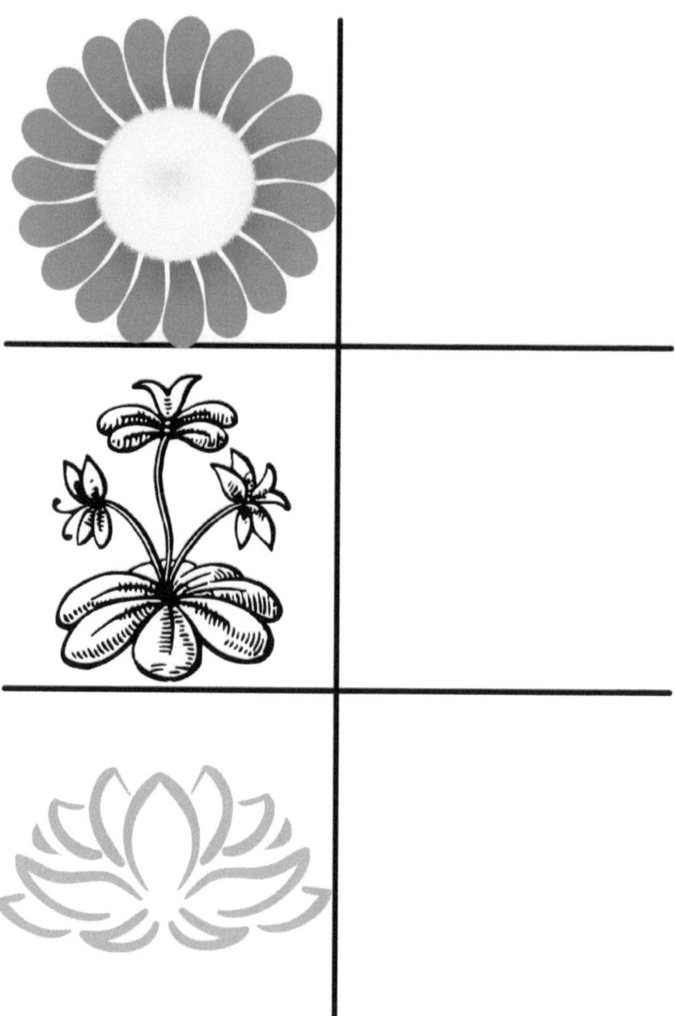

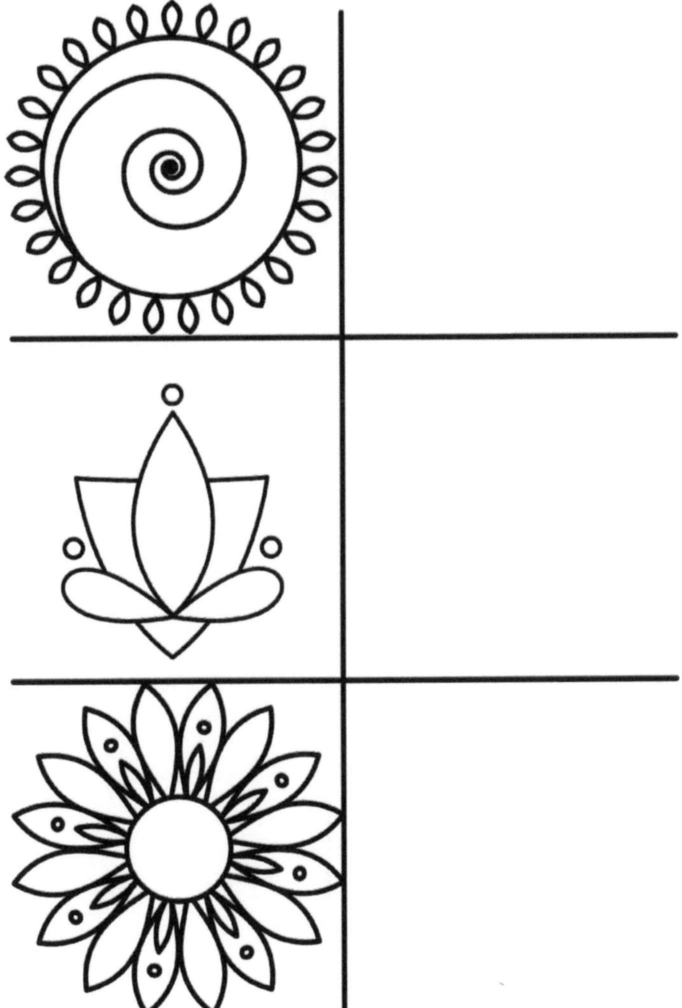

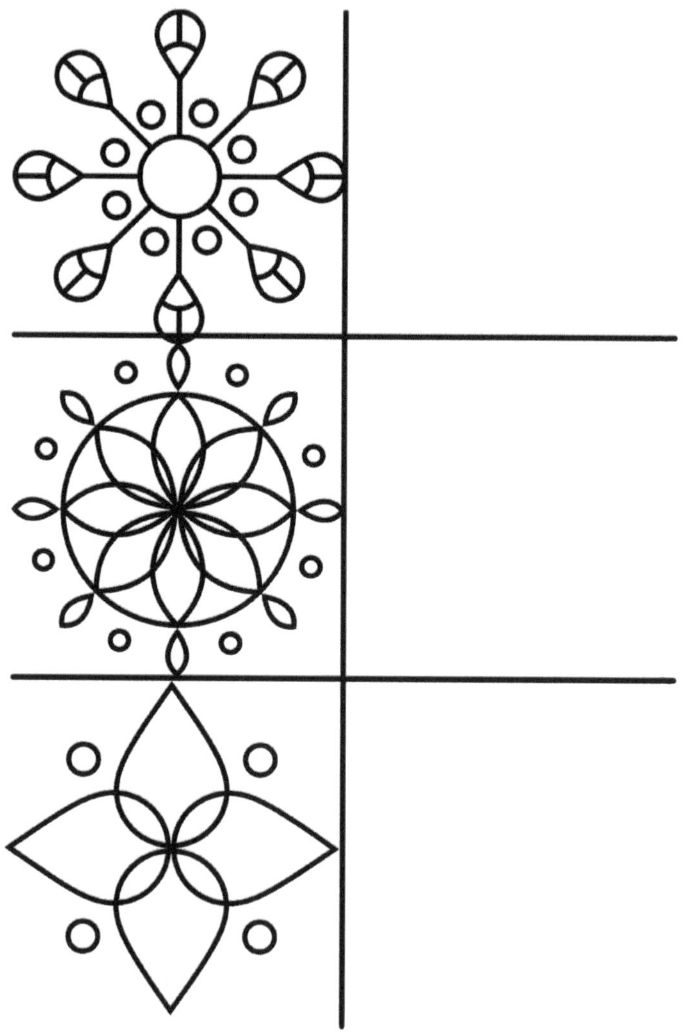

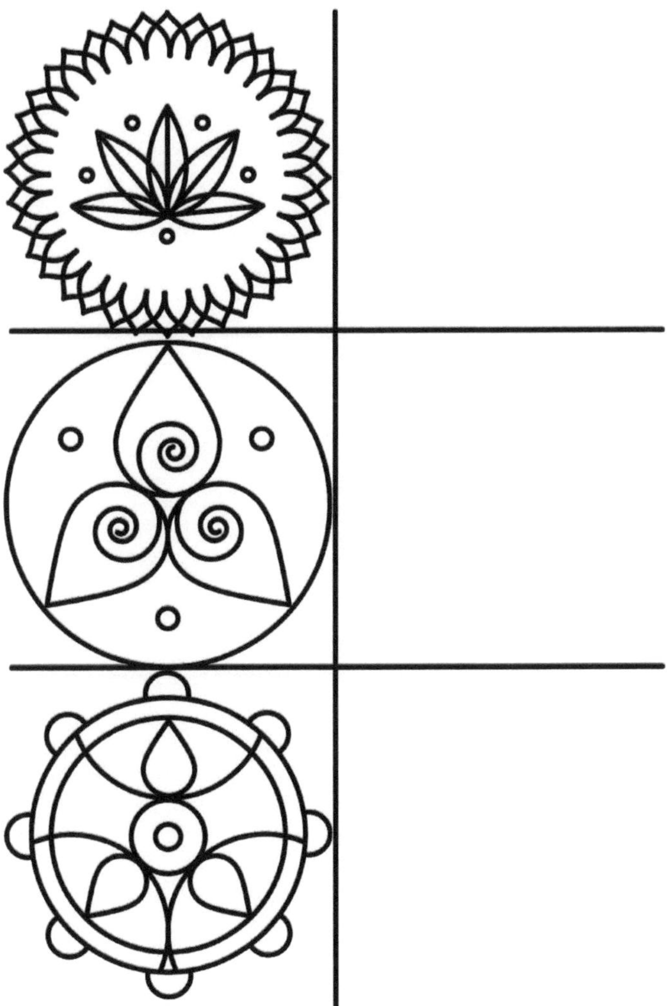

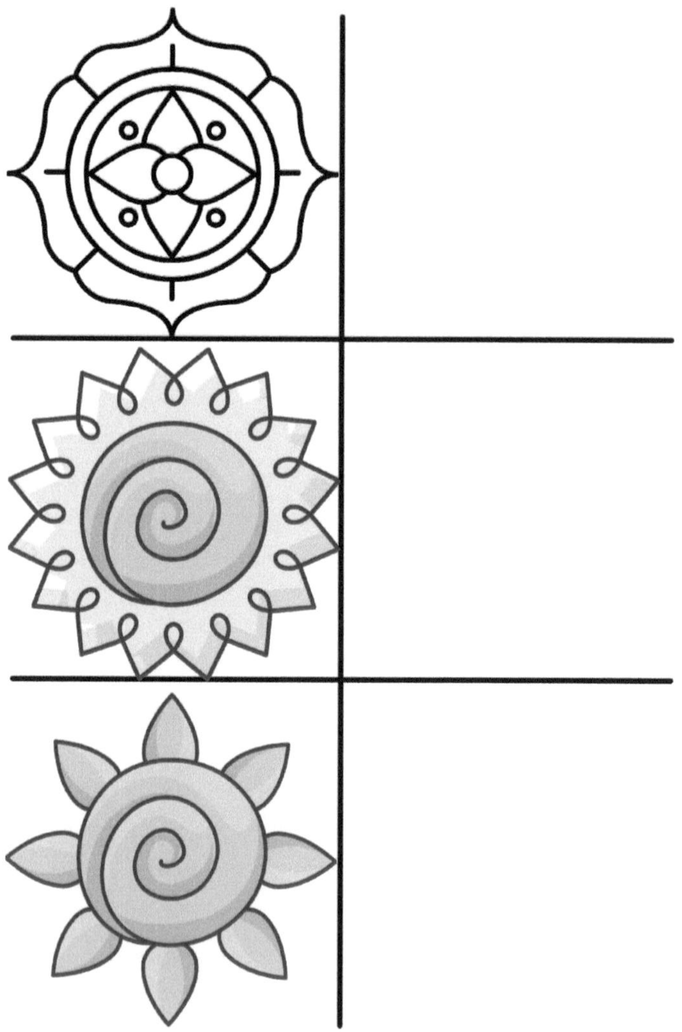

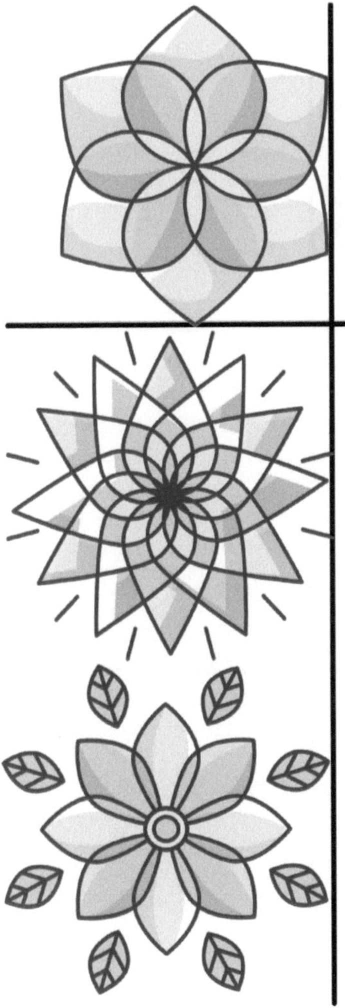

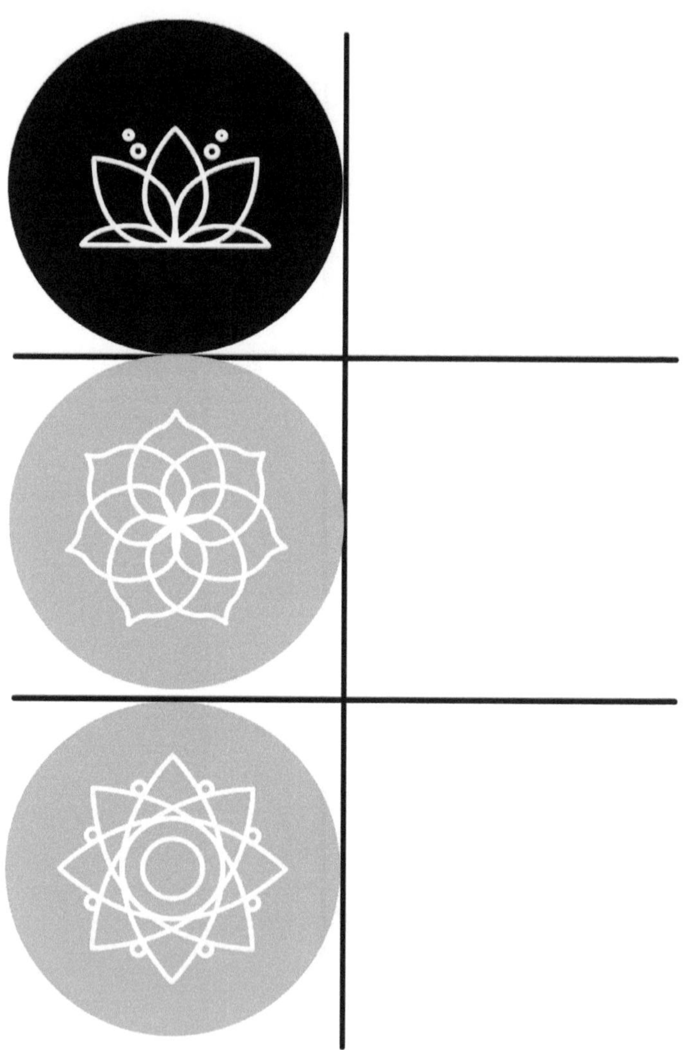

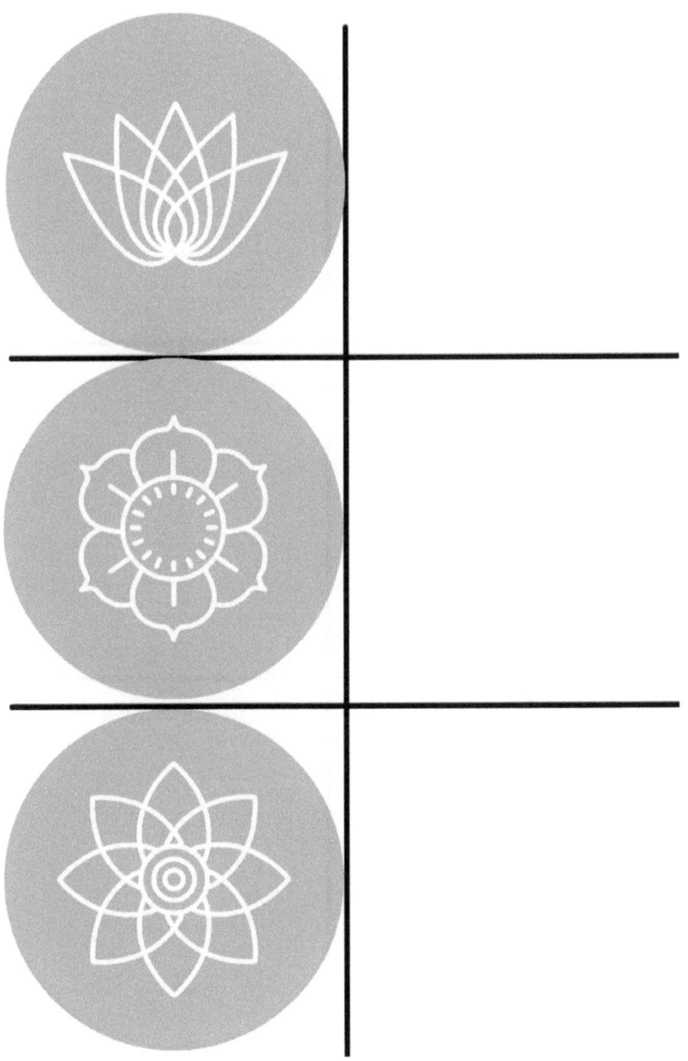

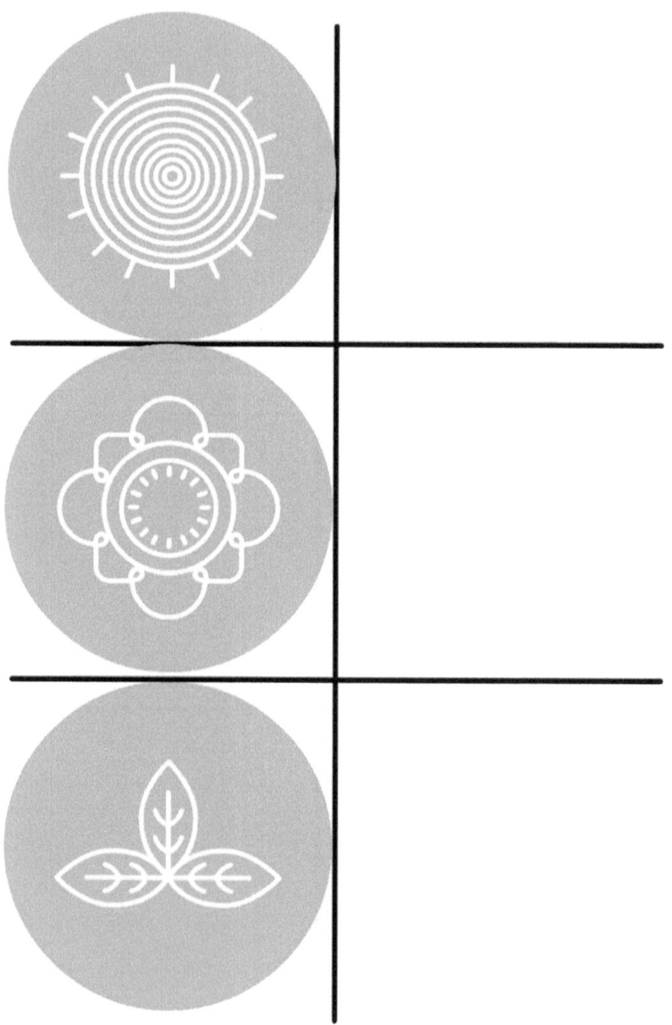

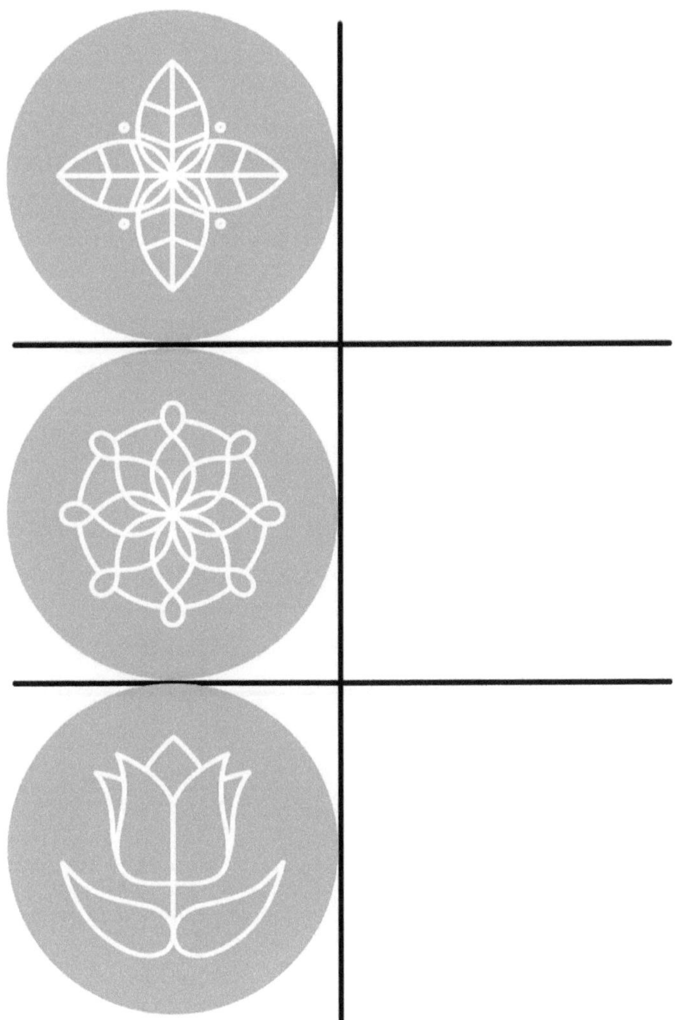

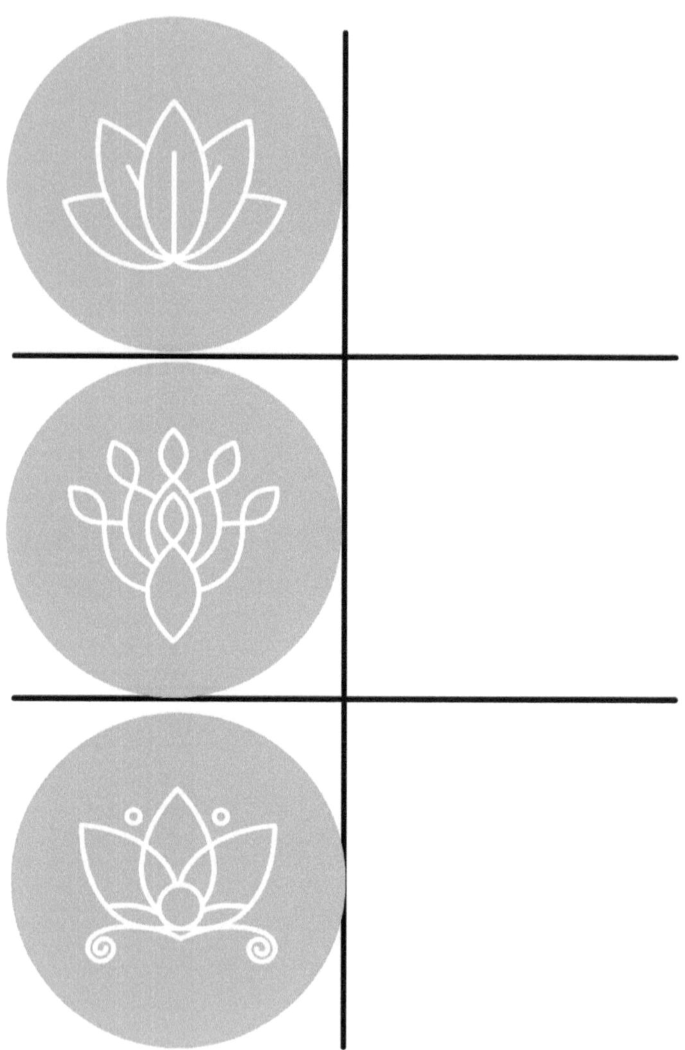

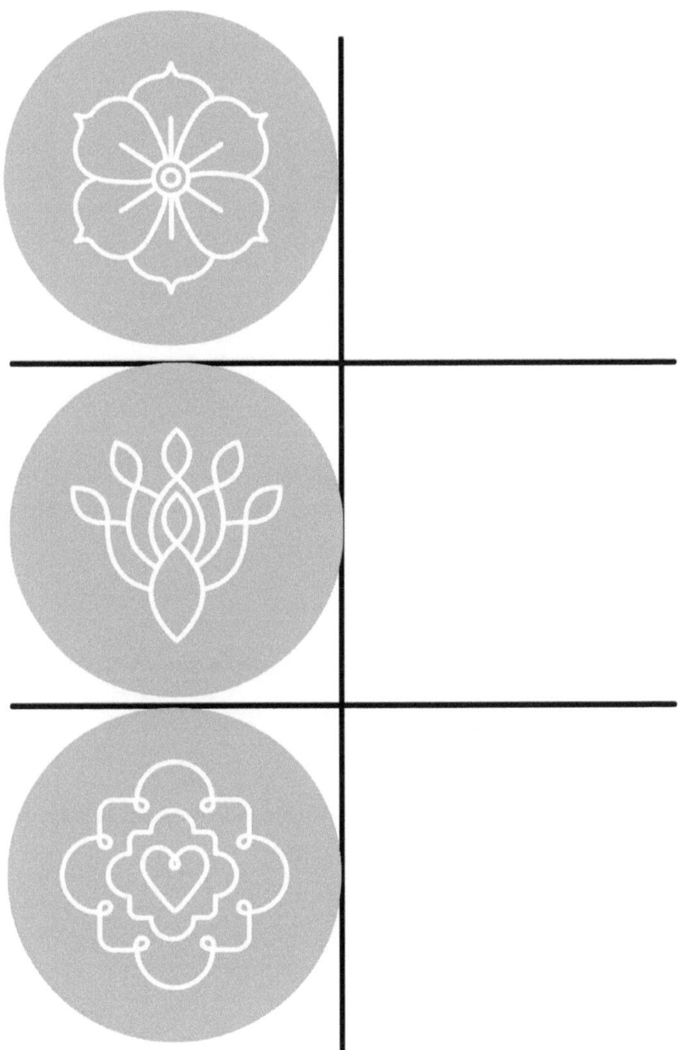

Draw the flowers that you know except the designs given in this book

Enter Caption

CHAPTER X

Patterns

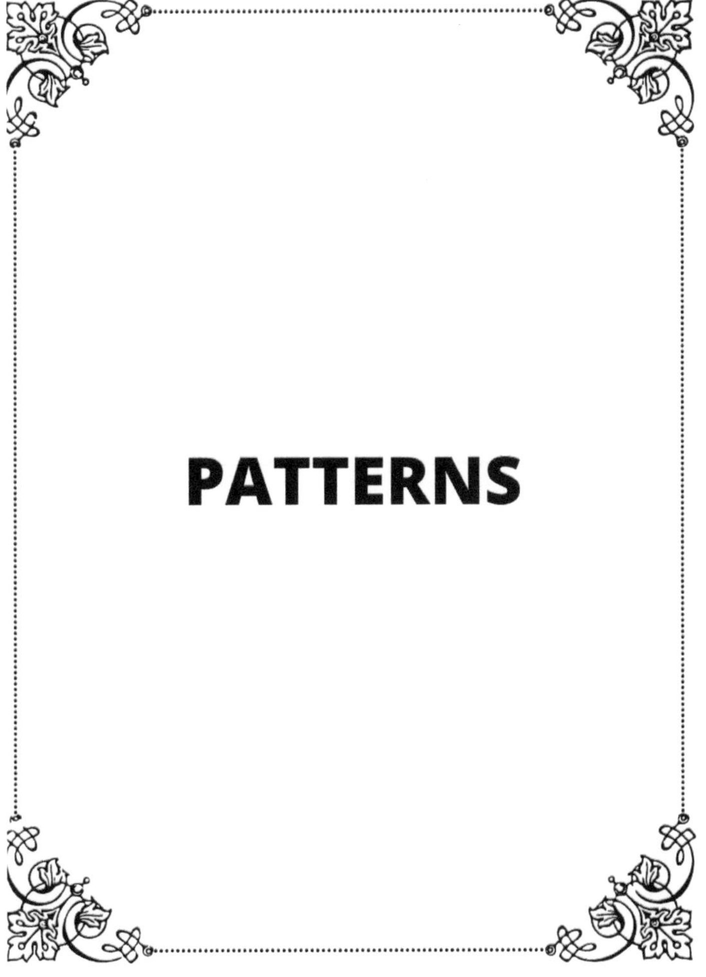

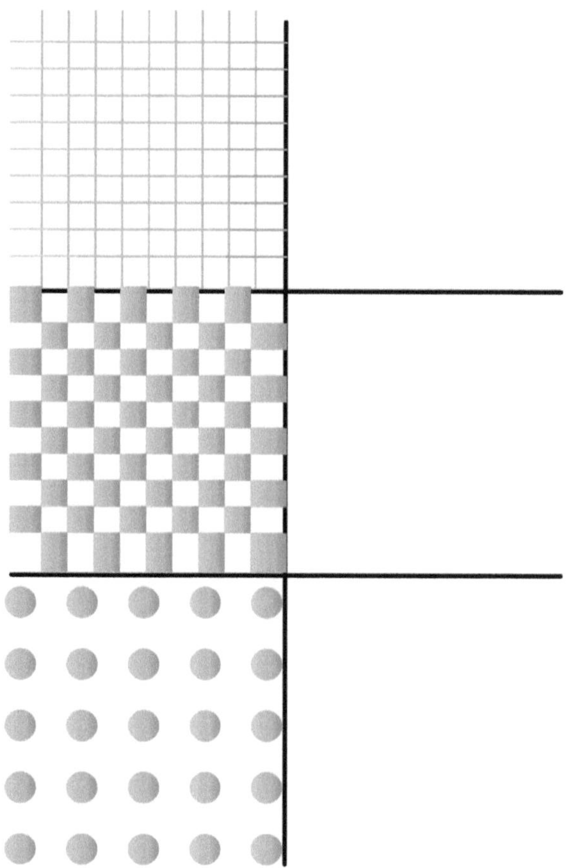

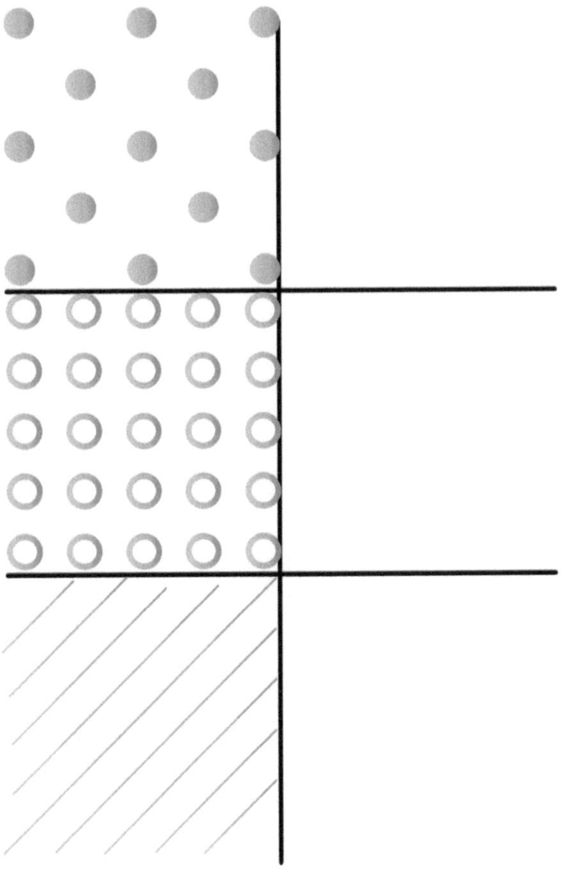

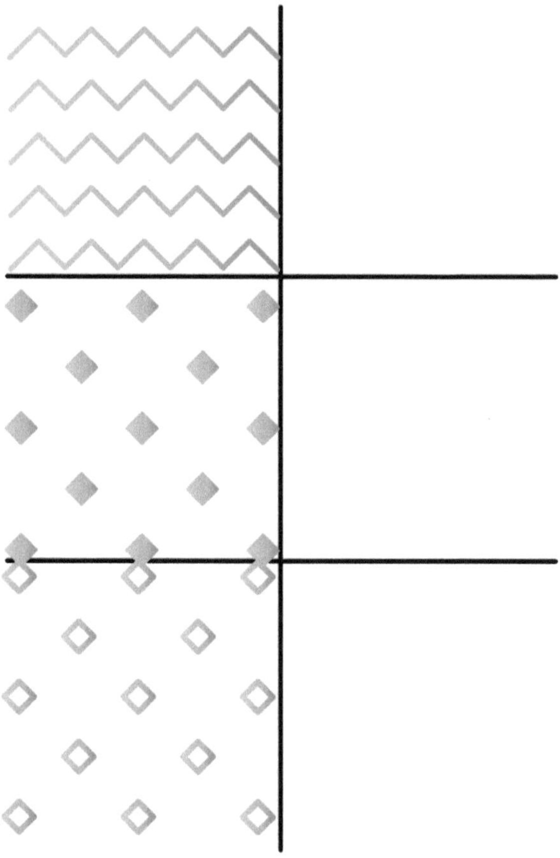

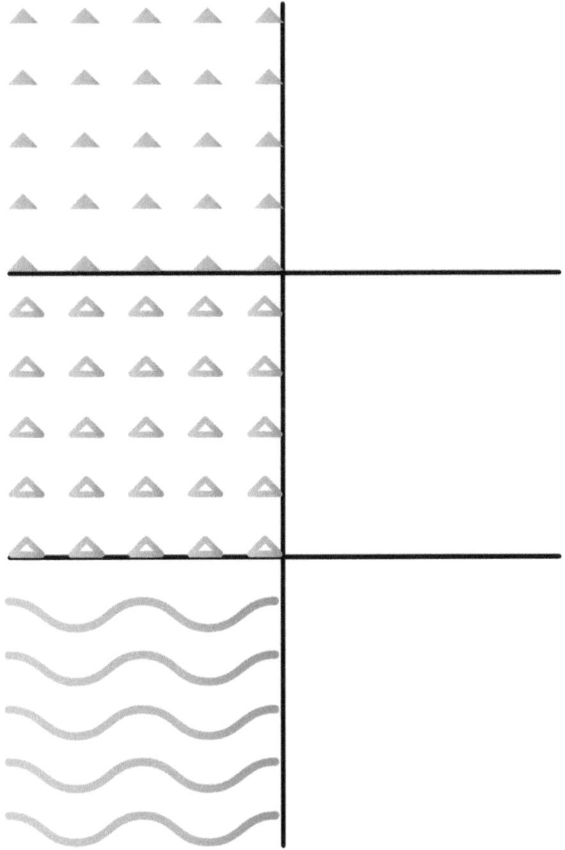

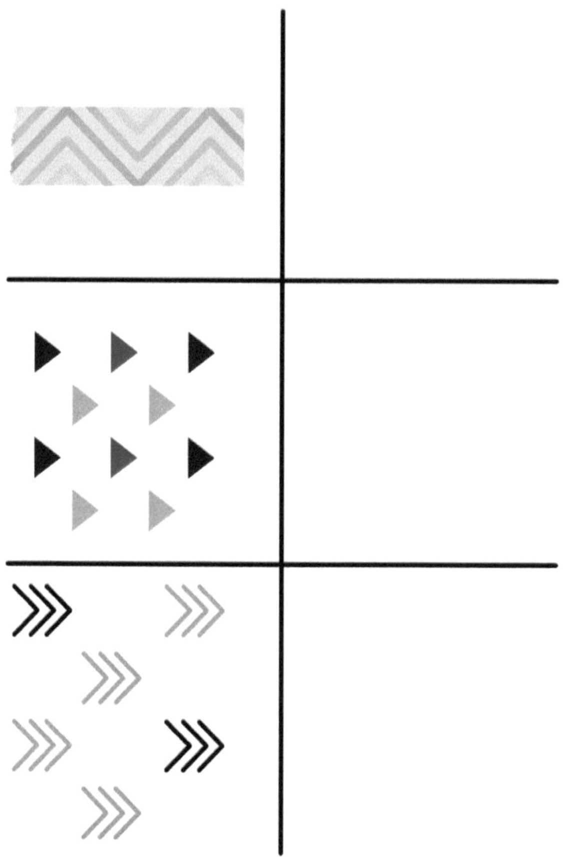

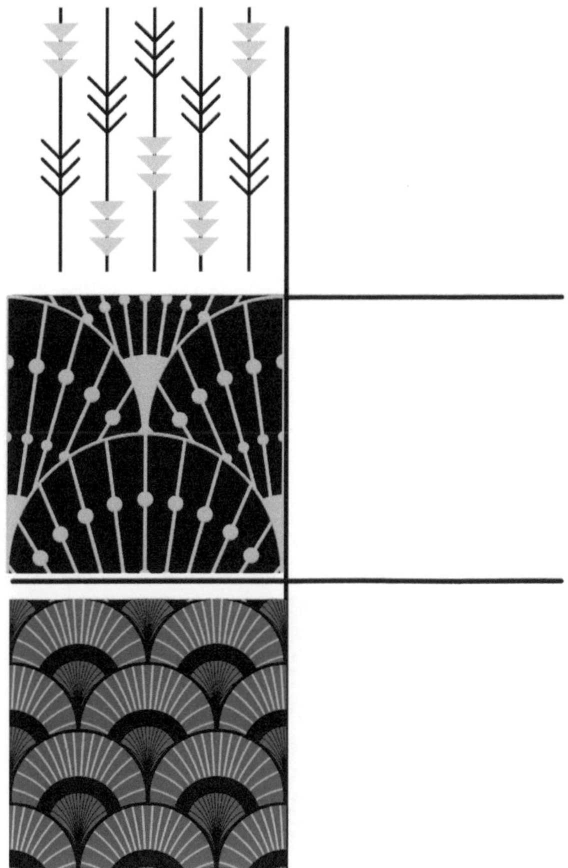

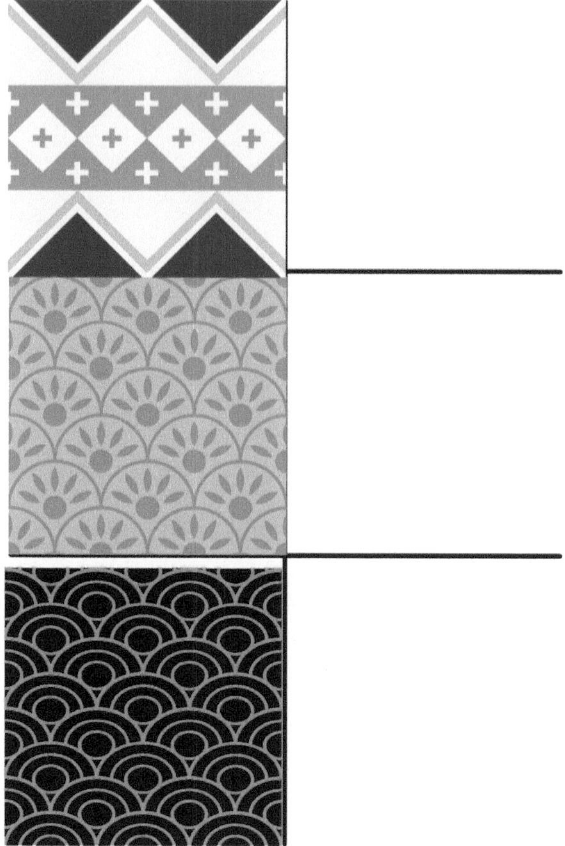

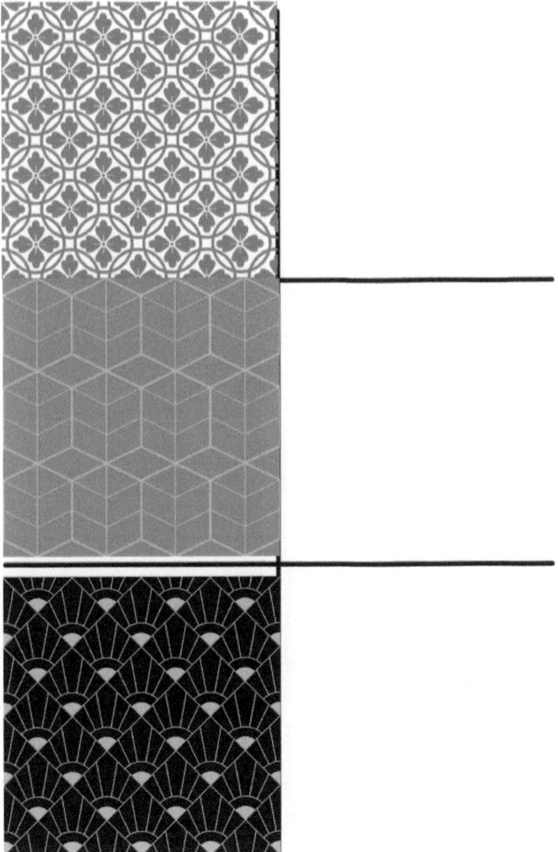

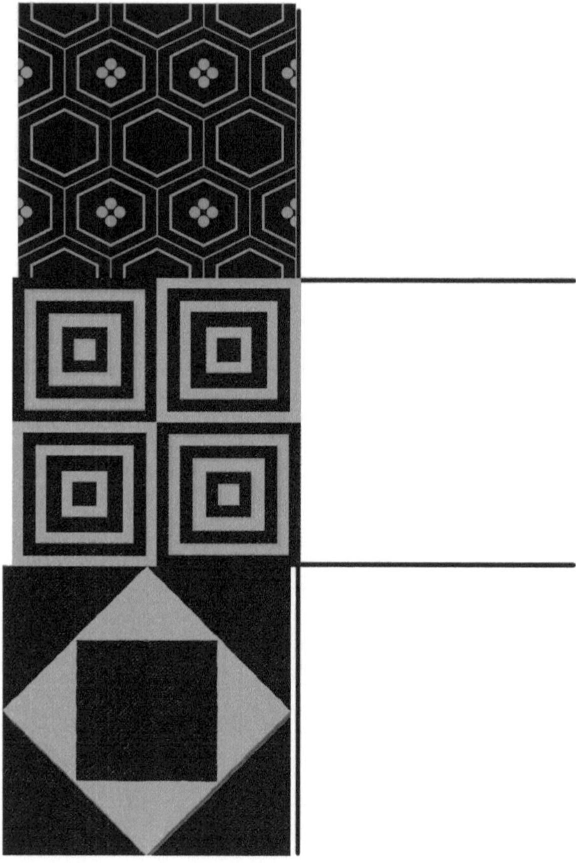

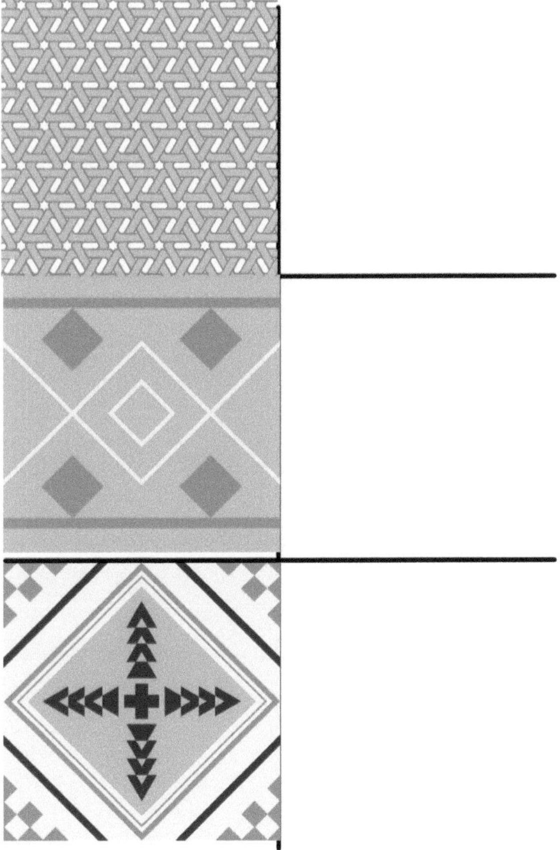

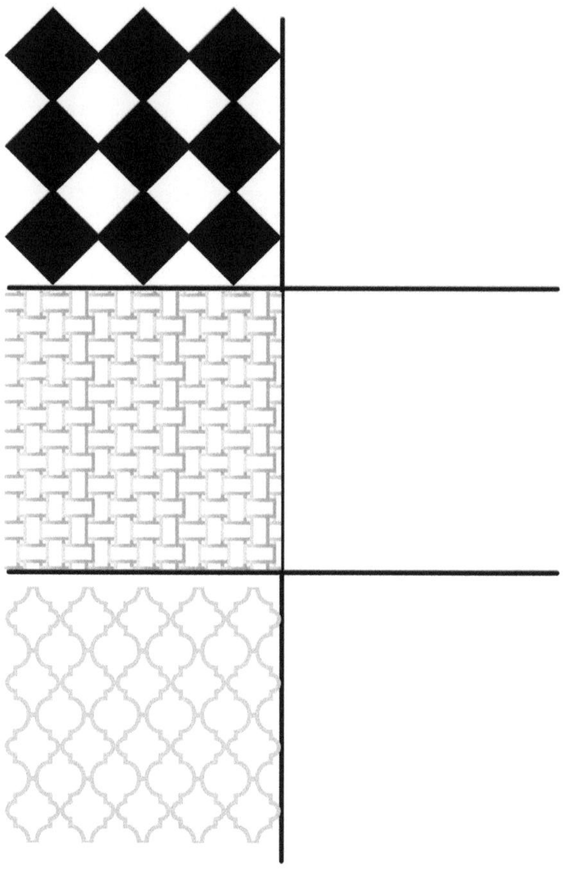

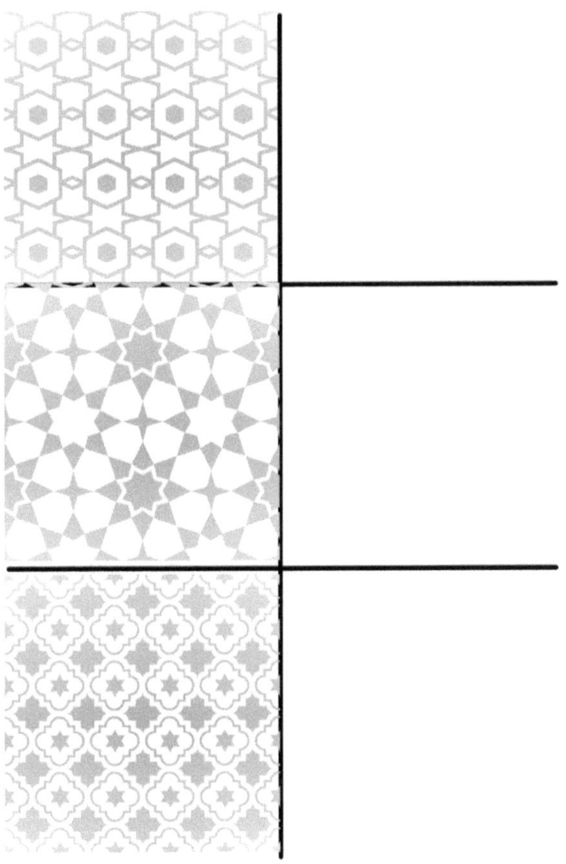

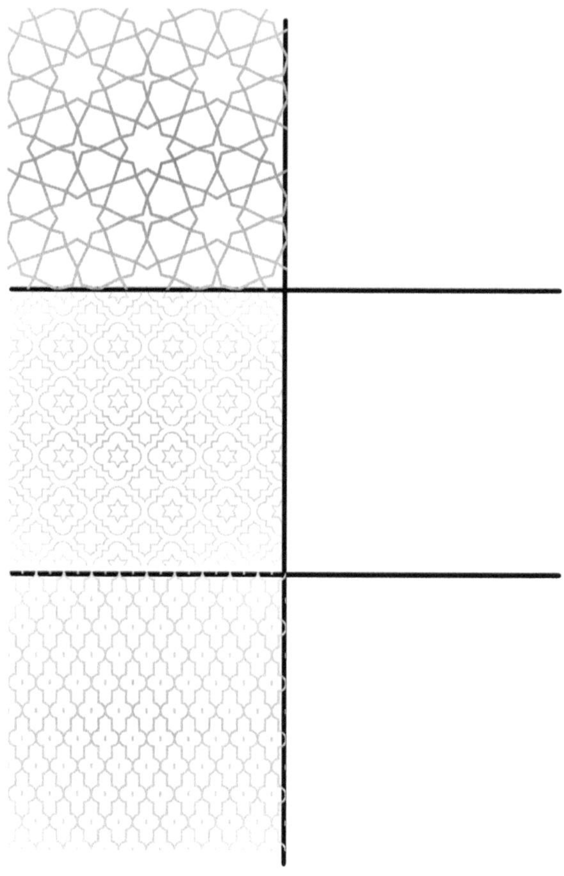

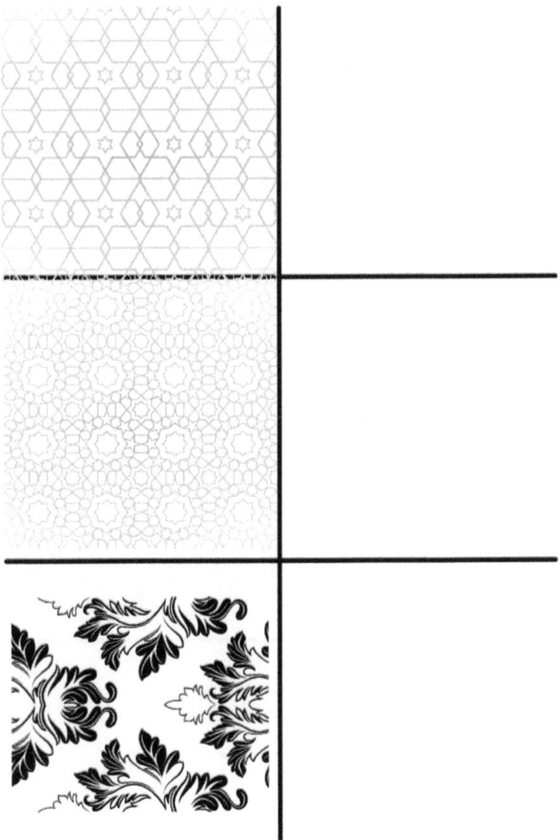

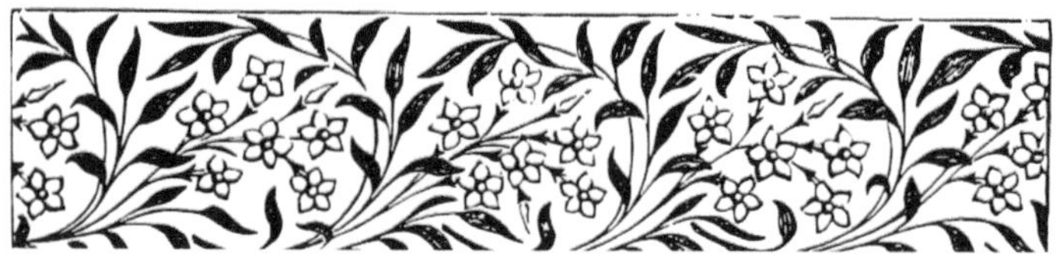

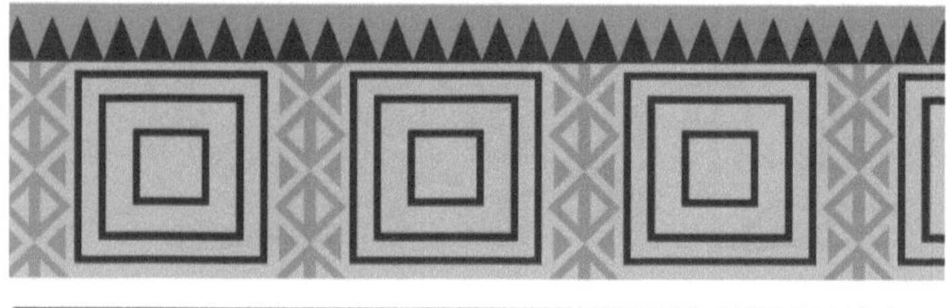

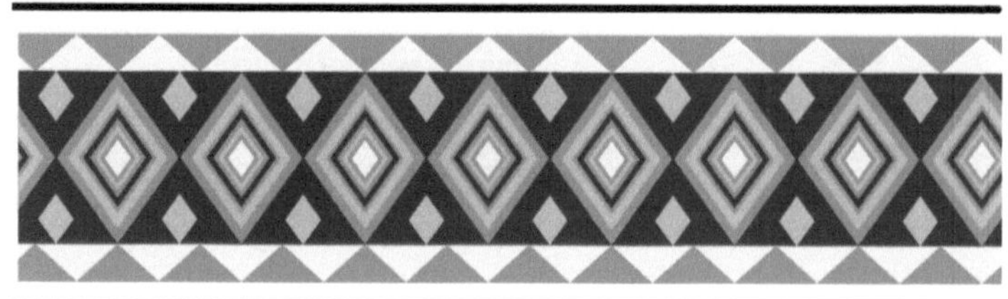

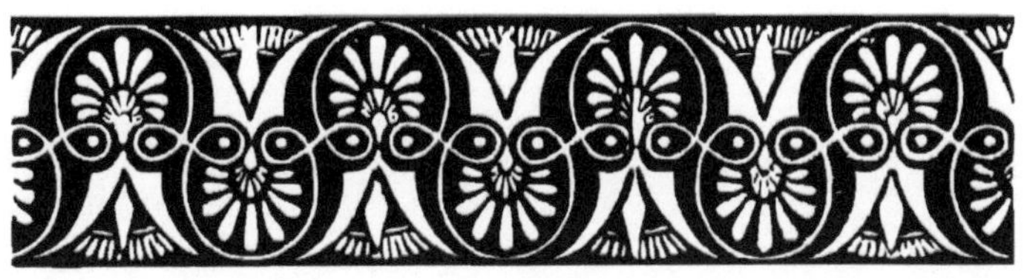

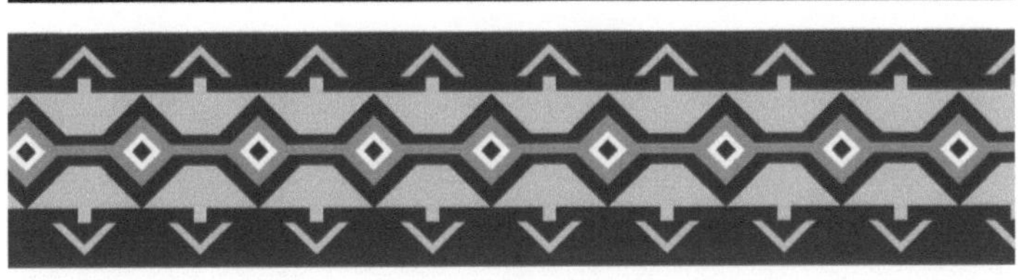

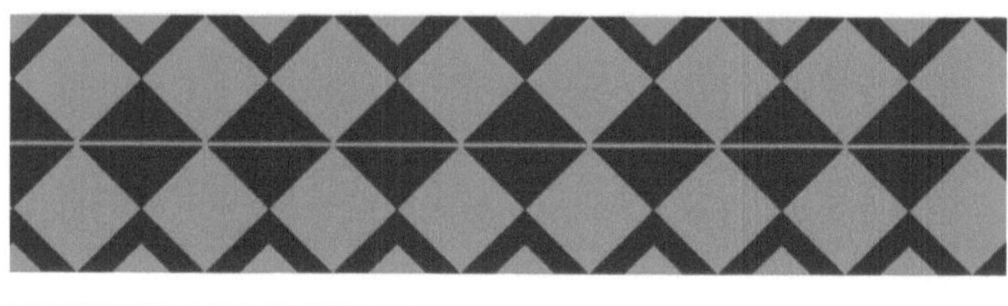

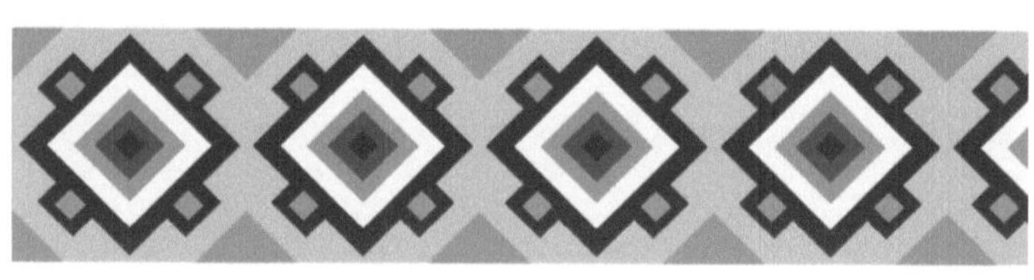

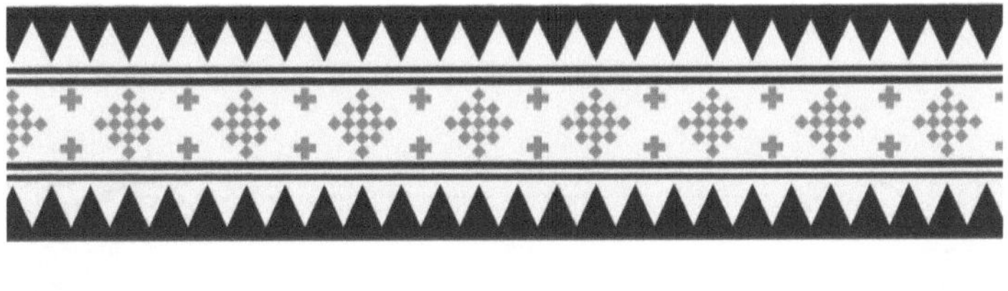

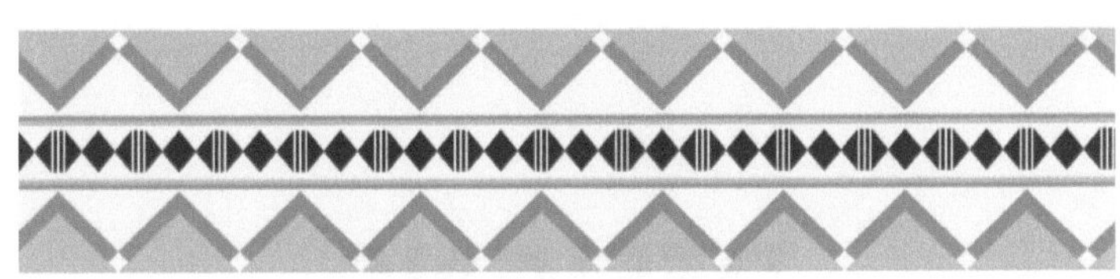

CHAPTER XI

Basic Designs

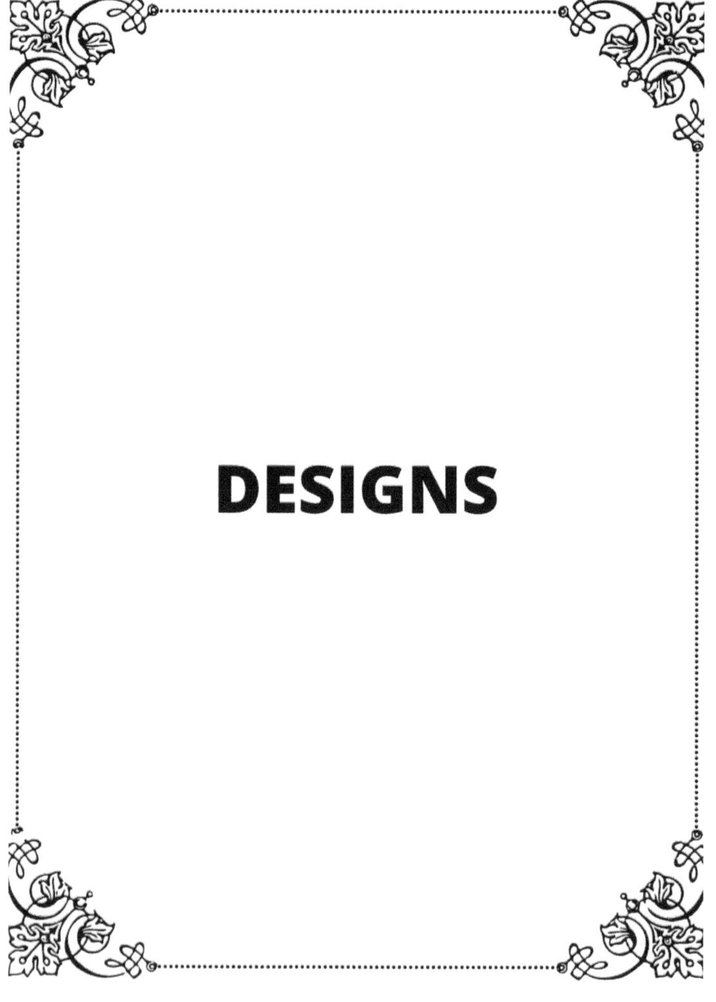

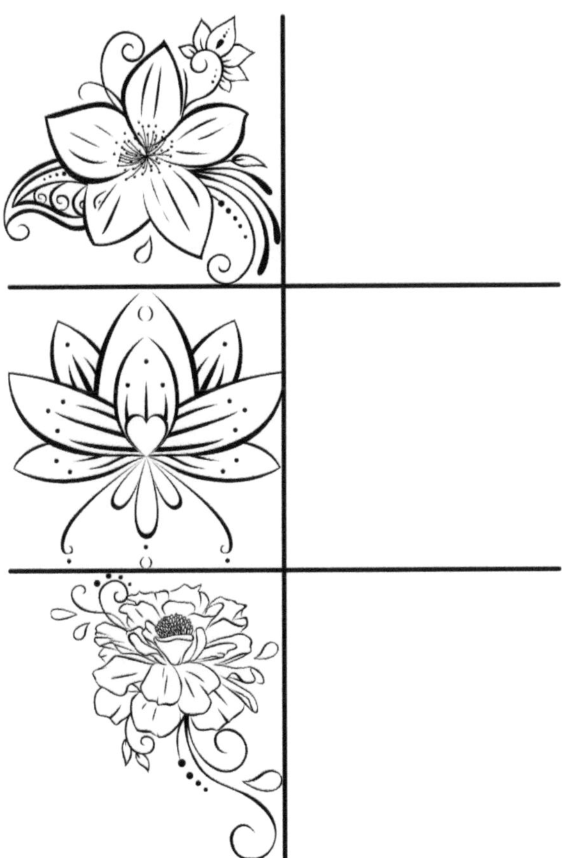

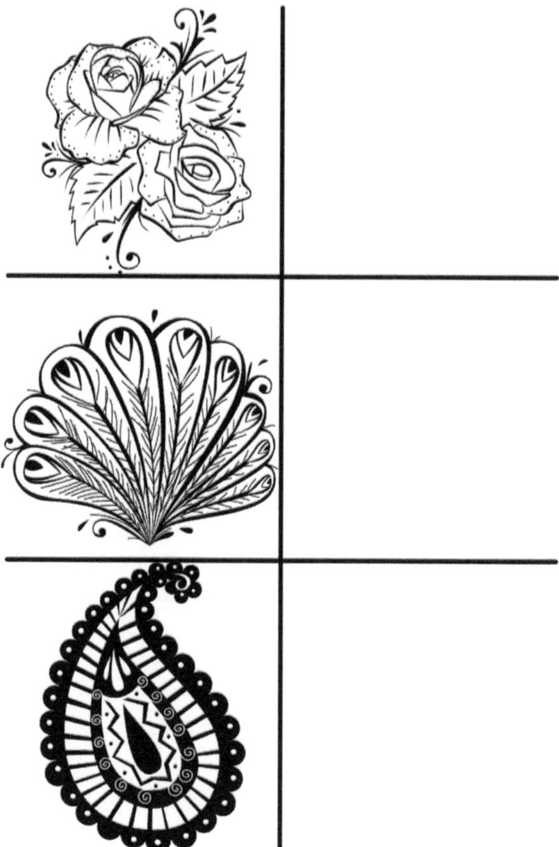

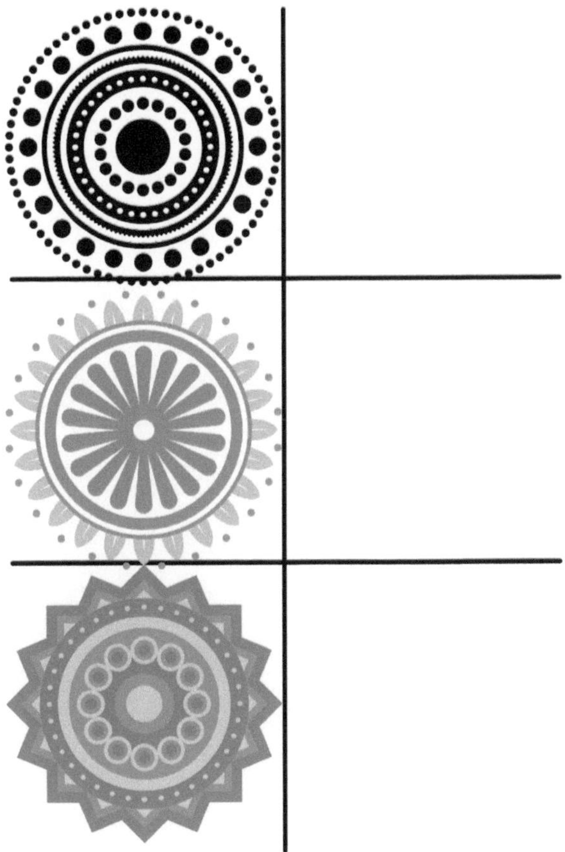

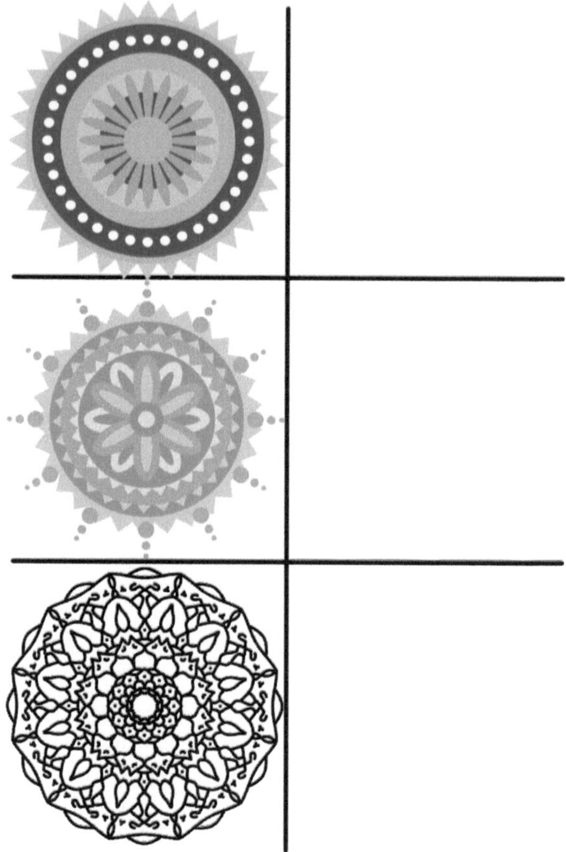

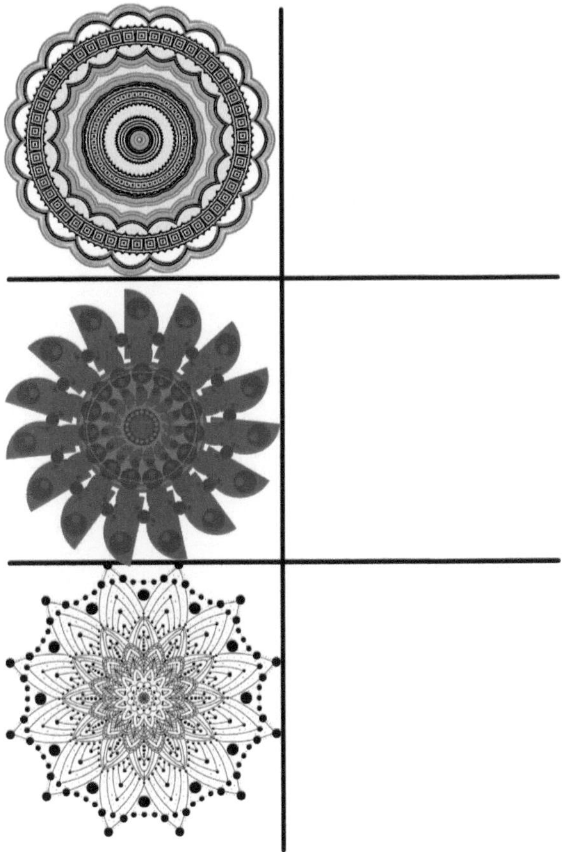

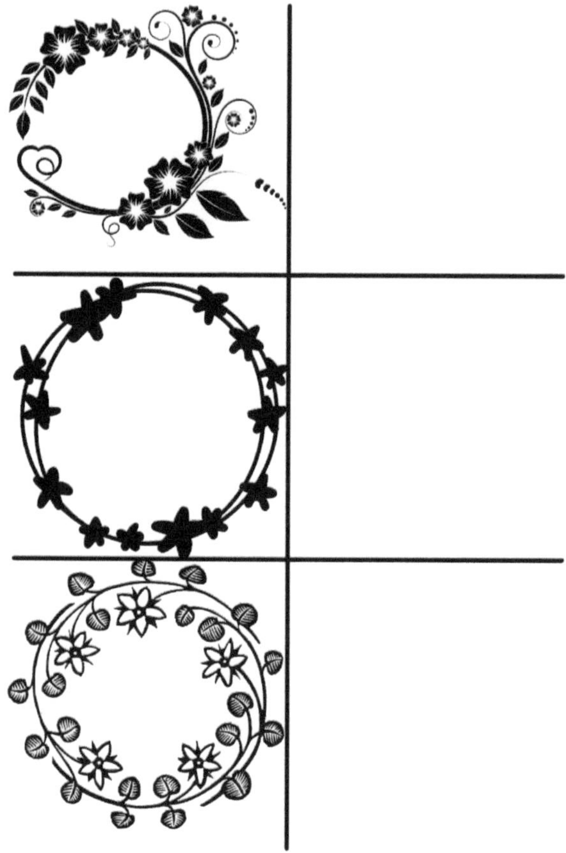

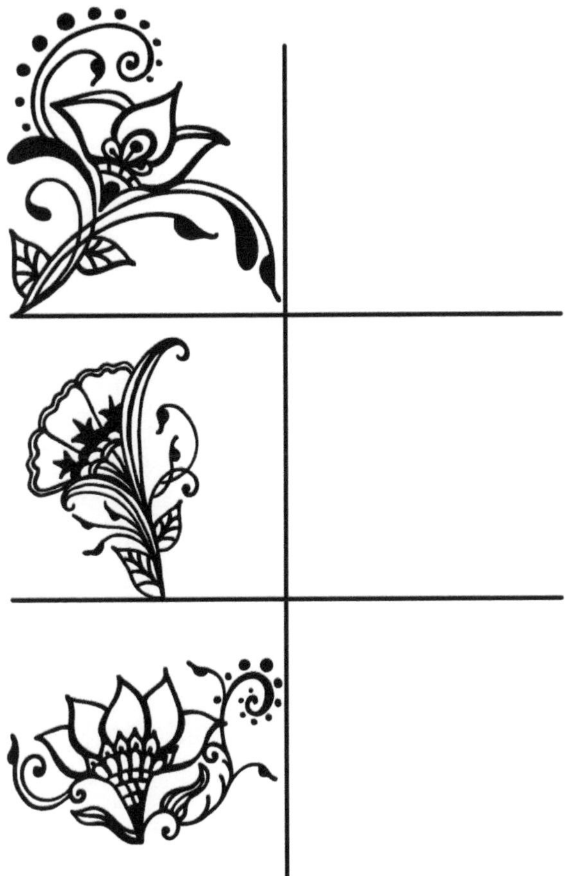

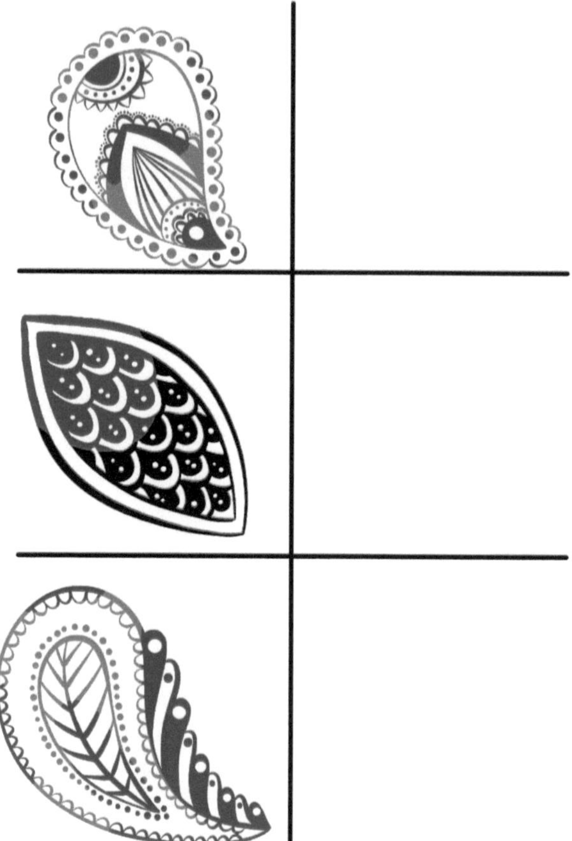

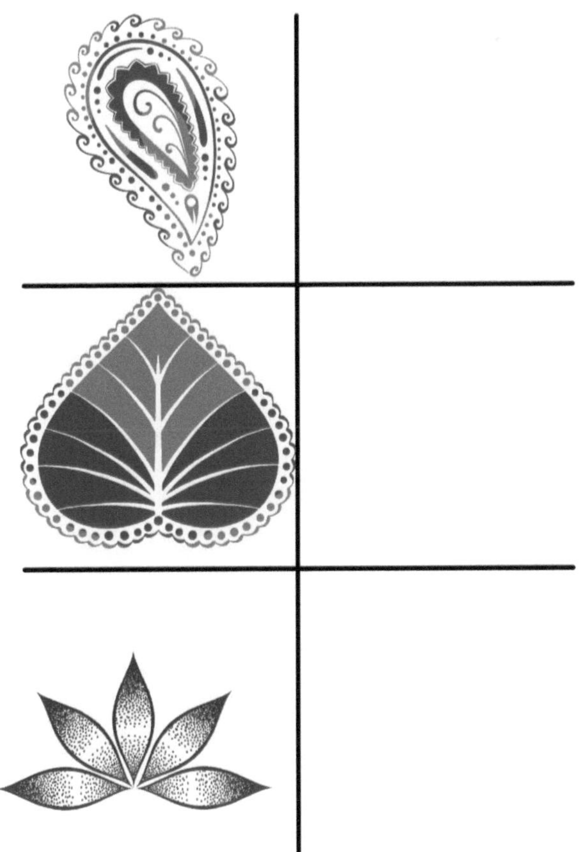

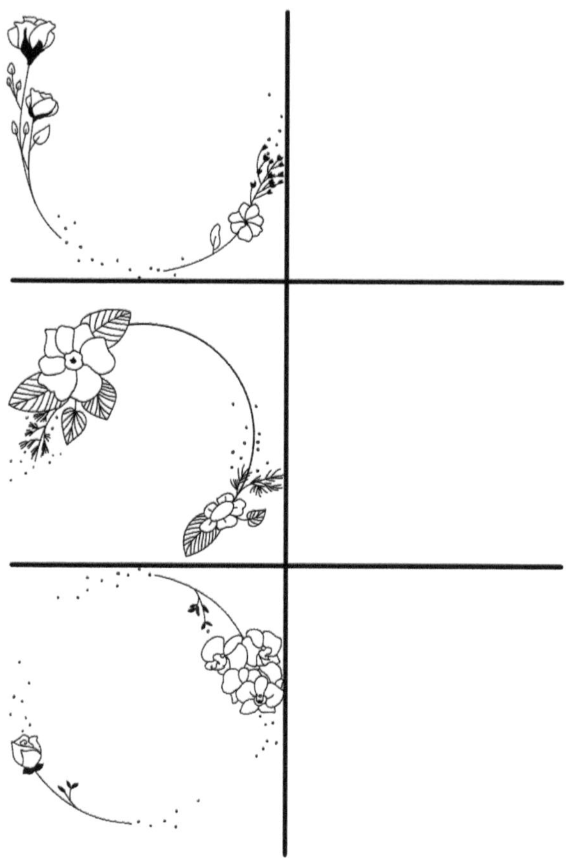

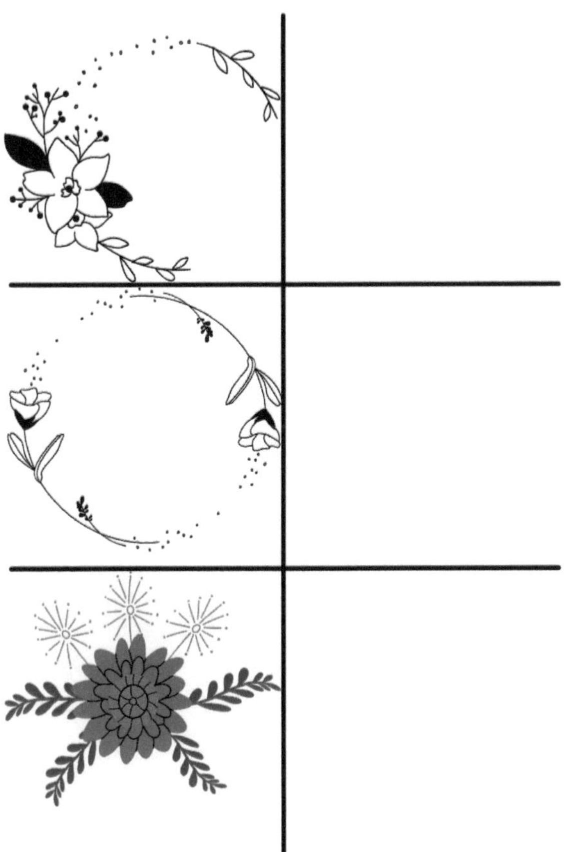

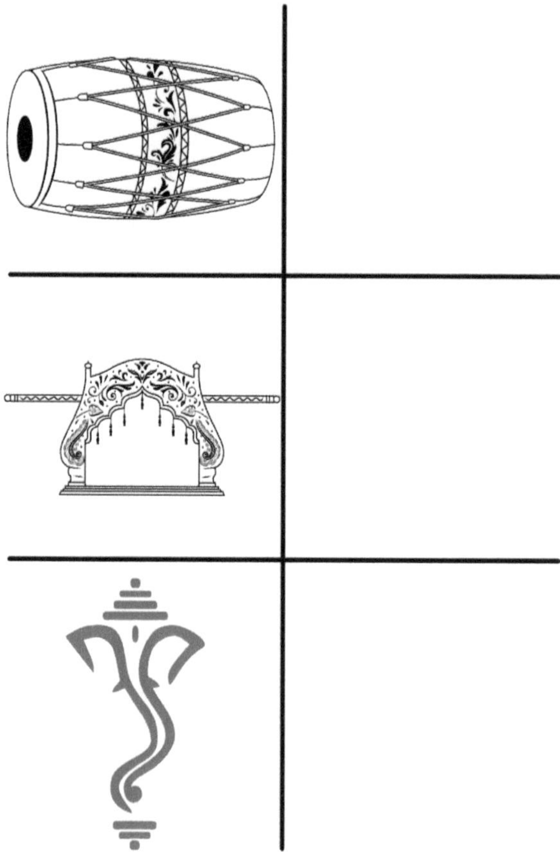

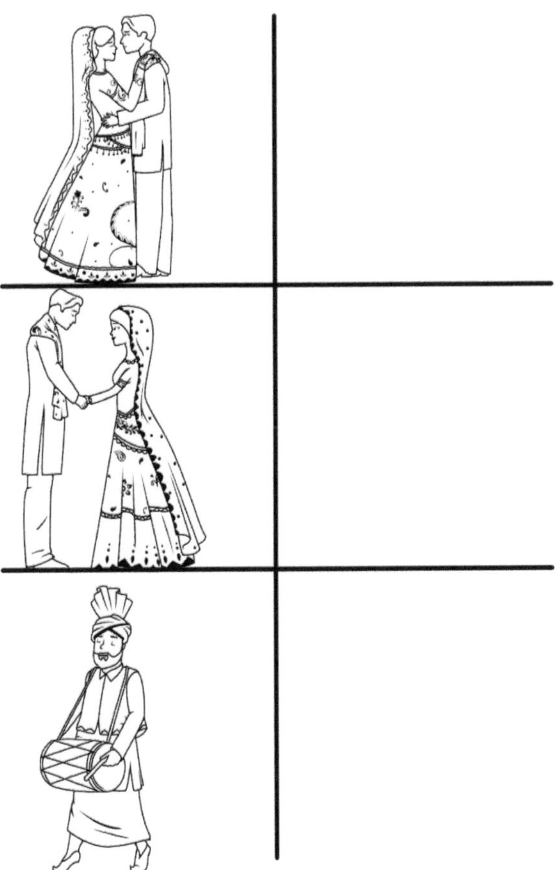

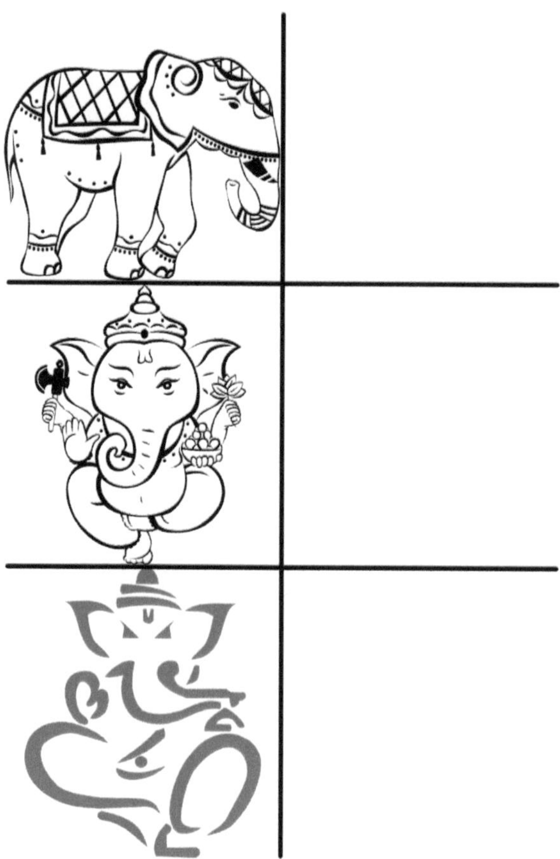

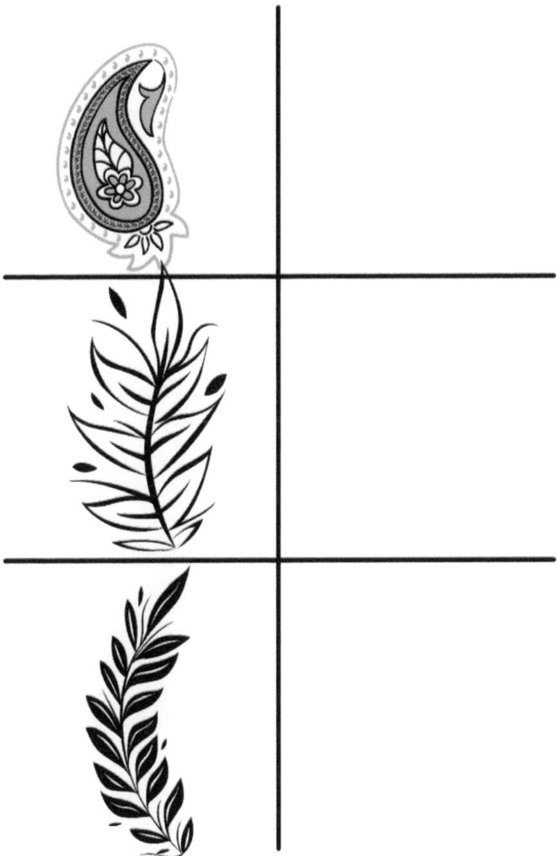

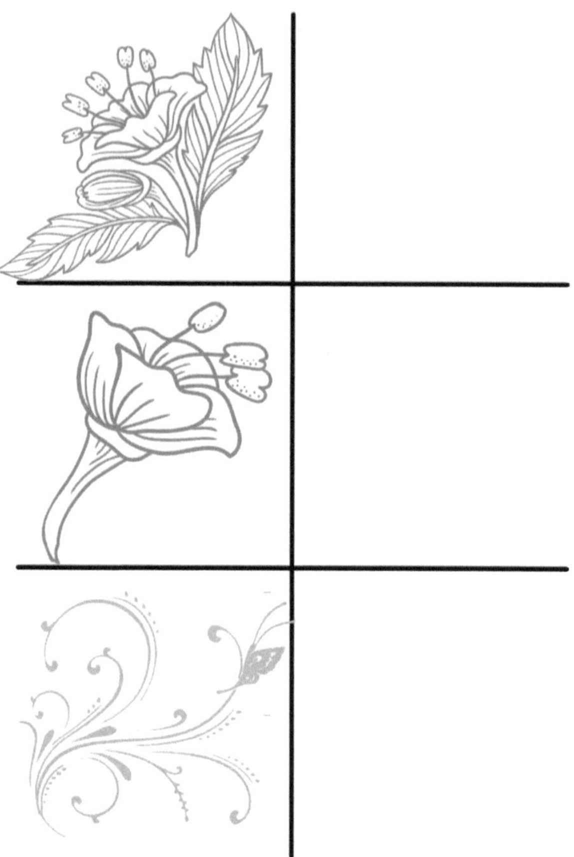

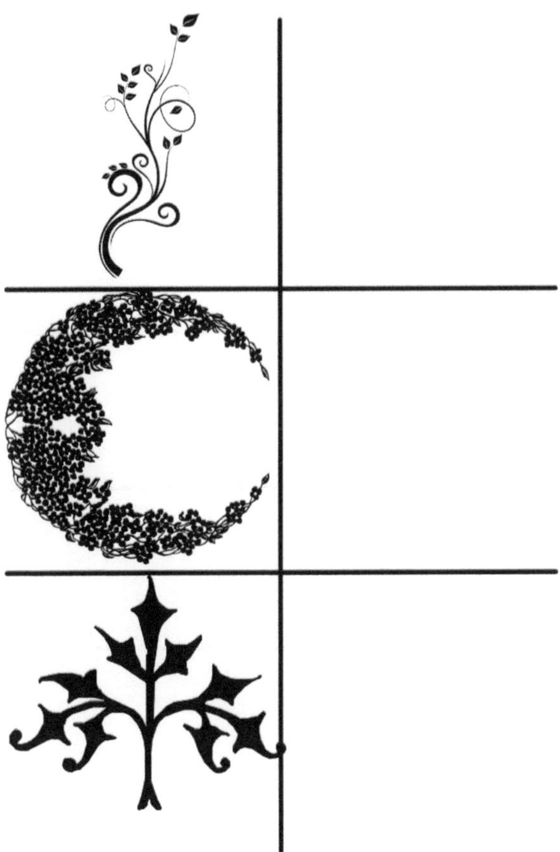

Certification

After completing the workbook please fill the form on the link https://forms.gle/gDM6prcPu5hUtTp88 to receive your certificate.

Follow us on Instagram @henna_design_world for daily updates of designs.

Do not forget to add hash tag #henna_design_world when you post henna design, selected designs will be featured on henna design world page.

Like us on facebook

www.ingramcontent.com/pod-product-compliance
Ingram Content Group UK Ltd.
Pitfield, Milton Keynes, MK11 3LW, UK
UKHW040010200726
13854UKWH00001B/124

9 798885 558235